I0439687

PROHIBITIONS, PRICE CAPS, AND DISCLOSURES:

A LOOK AT STATE POLICIES AND ALTERNATIVE FINANCIAL PRODUCT USE

Prepared for the US Department of the Treasury by the Urban Institute, 2010

Authors of this report are:

Signe-Mary McKernan, Urban Institute

Caroline Ratcliffe, Urban Institute

Daniel Kuehn, Urban Institute

Abstract

This study uses new nationally representative data from the National Financial Capability State-by-State Survey to examine the relationship between state-level alternative financial service (AFS) policies (prohibitions, price caps, disclosures) and consumer use of five AFS products: payday loans, auto title loans, pawn broker loans, refund anticipation loans, and rent-to-own transactions. Looking across products rather than at one product in isolation allows a focus on patterns and relationships across products. The results suggest that more stringent price caps and prohibitions are associated with lower product use and do not support the hypothesis that prohibitions and price caps on one AFS product lead consumers to use other AFS products.

Acknowledgments

This report was completed under contract to the U.S. Department of the Treasury Order Number GS23F8198H/T09BPA017, with funds authorized by the U.S. Department of the Treasury.

Oversight and review were provided by the Treasury Department's Office of Financial Education and Financial Access. The report benefited from the comments experience, and advice of Robert Lerman, Eugene Steuerle, and Douglas Wissoker. It also benefited from the project literature review completed by Brett Theodos and Jessica Compton. We owe a special thanks to the Financial Industry Regulatory Authority (FINRA), for making their data available.

The Urban Institute is a nonprofit, nonpartisan policy research and educational organization that examines the social, economic, and governance problems facing the nation. The views expressed are those of the authors and should not be attributed to the Urban Institute, its trustees, or its funders.

TABLE OF CONTENTS

I. INTRODUCTION

Annual revenues from alternative financial services (AFS) exceed $25 billion (Rivlin 2010)[1]. Millions of American households, especially households in the bottom half of the income distribution, use AFS loans to meet short-term needs. Short-term loans secured by automobiles, paychecks, and tax refunds have attracted attention because of their high price. Although often small in initial denominations, this type of credit can add up to significant debt burdens. Numerous states have put restrictions on the fees AFS providers can charge, which the industry says could eliminate such services. It is unclear whether consumers are better off without access to these short-term products.

This study examines the relationship between AFS policies and consumer use of AFS products. We examine five AFS products: payday loans, auto title loans, pawnshop loans, refund anticipation loans, and rent-to-own transactions. We examine the policies for each product alone as well as in conjunction with one another, because policies that restrict the availability of one product can affect consumer use of another product. For example, state policies that limit the availability of payday loans could lead consumers to turn to auto title loans when credit needs arise.

We use new individual-level survey data and state-level policy data to answer the following three research questions:

1. What is the relationship between state-level AFS policies and AFS use?

2. Are restrictions on one AFS product associated with increased use of other AFS products?

3. How are demographic and economic characteristics related to the use of AFS products?

In doing so we contribute to the literature by looking across five products rather than at one product in isolation. This allows us to examine patterns across products as well as whether there is any relationship between a state law on one AFS product and consumer use of another AFS product.

We find evidence that prohibitions and price caps are associated with a reduction in the supply of AFS products. Specifically, we find prohibiting payday loans is associated with a 35 percent decline in the use of payday loans. State prohibitions do not necessarily prevent all state residents from getting a payday loan, since people can get payday loans via the Internet or go across state lines to obtain the loan. We also find that price caps are associated with reduced use of auto title loans and pawnshop loans. Moving from no price cap on auto title loans to an annual percentage rate (APR) cap of 36 percent is associated with a 30 percent decline in auto

---

[1] In 2008, Pawnbrokers earned $4 billion in revenue, while payday lenders and rent-to-own businesses each earned $7 billion in revenue (Rivlin 2010).

title borrowing. Similarly, moving from no price cap on pawnshop loans to a monthly interest rate cap of 3 percent (roughly a 40 percent APR) is associated with a 25 percent decline in pawnshop borrowing. We also examine disclosure requirements for refund anticipation loans and renting to own and find little evidence that these requirements are related to AFS product use. Our findings may be a result of data limitations, as other studies suggest that clear and timely disclosures reduce AFS product use.

Finally, our results do not support the hypothesis that prohibitions and price caps on one AFS product lead consumers to use other AFS products. This last result does not necessarily convert to a universal rule, since demand for alternatives would depend upon the specific restrictions imposed and how readily the substitute is available. For instance, in a related paper, Theodos et al. (2010) find that restrictions on the use of refund anticipation loans by the military did lead to large substitution of the cheaper but related refund anticipation checks. Refund anticipation loans and checks are often sold by the same vendor or tax preparation firm, although refund anticipation checks are payment rather than credit products.

The rest of the paper is organized as follows. Section II provides an overview of the five products and summarizes key findings from the literature. Section III provides a conceptual framework for thinking about how state policies might affect AFS product use. The data and empirical model are described in Sections IV and V, respectively. Section VI presents the empirical results, answering each of the three research questions in turn. Finally, Section VII discusses policy implications and Section VIII provides a summary and conclusion.

II. BACKGROUND AND LITERATURE

Overview of the Five AFS Products

One third of low-income families without savings accounts report that they would use a payday lender or pawn something to pay a large bill in an emergency (McKernan and Ratcliffe 2008). Payday, pawnshop, and auto title lenders all tender small loans intended to carry borrowers through temporary cash shortages. Payday lenders, for example, provide short-term loans to working people with bank accounts. The typical payday loan is for roughly $250–$300 for two weeks, with fees of $15–$20 per $100 borrowed (Flannery and Samolyk 2005). Pawnshop and auto title lenders also provide short-term loans but use collateral (such as jewelry or a car title) to secure them. Pawnbroker loans are typically a one-month loan under $100 (National Pawnbrokers Association 2008), and the typical auto title loan is a one-month loan between $600 and $2,500 (South Carolina Appleseed Legal Justice Center 2004).

Refund anticipation loans and rent-to-own stores provide quick access to tax refunds and merchandise, respectively. Refund anticipation loans are short-term loans secured by a taxpayer's anticipated income tax refund. Taxpayers receive their tax refunds more quickly through refund anticipation loans—within a few days rather than the eight weeks it can take to

3

receive a paper check refund. Refund anticipation loans are often used to pay for pressing financial needs and tax preparation fees (Theodos et al. 2010). Rent-to-own transactions are self-renewing weekly or monthly leases for merchandise (e.g., furniture) with the option to purchase. At the end of each lease period, consumers have the option to return the merchandise or to continue to rent by paying for an additional lease period. Consumers can purchase the merchandise by renting to term (usually 18 to 24 months) or by early payment of a proportion (usually 50 percent to 60 percent) of the remaining lease payments.

What We Know from the Literature

The literature on AFS is substantial,[2] but only a small subset of this literature examines the relationship between AFS policies and AFS product use. The majority of the AFS literature focuses on payday loans, while there is an important gap in the literature for other AFS products. The literature has several important findings that are relevant to this paper. First, some AFS suppliers circumvent state laws. Second, binding price caps and prohibitions have been found to reduce supply. Third, AFS consumers have relatively few alternatives to AFS products and so, fourth, are not necessarily better off without AFS products. Fifth, well-designed and -timed disclosures can affect consumer behavior for some but not all consumers. Sixth, fee disclosures may be better than APR disclosures.

Some AFS suppliers circumvent state laws. Fox and Guy (2005) find that auto title lenders use several loan structures to avoid state usury or small-loan rate caps. Some lenders size their loans to fall outside rate-cap limits. In South Carolina, for example, auto title loans are called 601 loans because the threshold for small loan rate caps is $600. In other states, auto title lenders repackage single-payment title loans as lines of credit to get around rate caps or make loans via the Internet to avoid rate caps (by using laws from states with no rate caps). Similarly, Feltner (2007) finds that nearly all the loans referenced in 61 Illinois court cases (of auto title borrowers who were taken to court in 2005 by a licensed auto title company) had terms of more than 60 days, allowing them to circumvent strong consumer protection laws passed by the state in 2001.

Stegman (2007) notes that payday lenders are developing methods of circumventing restrictions, including the use of credit service organizations (CSOs) that allow payday providers to operate as loan facilitators for third-party lenders, which are not subject to state or federal regulation. Even more recently, payday providers have been charging "participation fees," which provide borrowers with the right to take out loans at interest rates that fall within state limits. Payday provider profits are thus earned through participation fees, rather than high interest rates. Stegman (2007) notes that there is little evidence indicating whether these recent innovations have enabled payday lenders to avoid existing restrictions.

---

[2] See Caskey (1994) and Barr (2004) for seminal overviews of alternative financial services and Theodos and Compton (2010) for a recent summary of the literature.

Skiba and Tobacman (2007) suggest that AFS lenders have an incentive to circumvent restrictions, because payday lenders do not earn excessive profits[3] and so would have a hard time absorbing the costs of restrictions. Contrary to popular belief, they find that payday lenders have profit rates that are comparable to traditional returns in the financial sector.

Binding price caps and prohibitions are likely to reduce supply. If there are no excessive profits in AFS products, then binding price caps are likely to reduce supply. Dunham (forthcoming 2010) finds that a 36 percent APR price cap on payday lending—such as the federal law for all military service members—causes payday lenders to lose money, so that they stop making payday loans. Flannery and Samolyk (2005) also find no evidence of excessive profits in payday lending. Prager (2009) finds that limitations on the rates payday suppliers can charge are associated with fewer payday lending stores per capita. The highest concentration of payday lending stores on a per capita basis are in those Southern states that do not explicitly or effectively prohibit payday lending—Alabama, South Carolina, Tennessee, Mississippi, and Louisiana. And Zinman (2010) finds that after a binding 2007 payday lending price cap took effect in Oregon, payday lenders exited Oregon and borrowing fell.

Stegman (2007) notes that one unintended consequence of driving payday lenders out of business with restrictions is that it could reduce price competition between lenders and raise prices. In other words, supply reduction can have the effect of conferring market power, particularly for providers able to circumvent restrictions.

AFS consumers have relatively few alternatives. Elliehausen and Lawrence (2001) find that a large percentage of AFS customers previously considered obtaining funds from traditional creditors, depository institutions, and finance companies. However, many other payday customers perceived limitations in credit availability and had fewer alternatives than the population as a whole. Stegman (2007) speculates that the lack of alternatives to AFS products may be related to reputation risks perceived by traditional banks and high fixed costs. Zinman (2010) finds that when payday borrowing fell in Oregon after the state price cap, former payday borrowers partially substituted bank overdrafts and late bill payment for payday lending. This substitution does not necessarily improve consumer well-being,[4] as research suggests that payday loans are preferable to overdraft protection plans (Fellowes and Mabanta 2008).

Consumers are not necessarily better off without AFS products, because they have few alternatives. Zinman (2010) investigates whether restricting access to expensive credit through

---

[3] Skiba and Tobacman (2007) assess AFS lender returns by comparing them to average S&P 500 returns and find that they are largely comparable. "Excessive profits" thus refers to profits in excess of typical returns.

[4] "Consumer well-being" is defined differently by different authors. For example, Melzer (forthcoming) uses a set of well-being survey measures from a nationally representative household survey. Fellowes and Mabanta (2008) frame the impact of AFS products on consumer well-being as a function of the potential wealth that is foregone when consumers use these products. Throughout this paper, the term will be used in a general sense to reflect various measures of household financial security.

the 2007 Oregon payday lending price cap helps consumers by preventing overborrowing. He finds the shift into plausibly inferior substitutes (bank overdrafts and late bill payment) and a deterioration in additional measures of financial condition are consistent with "restricted access harming, not helping, consumers on average" (abstract). Dunham (forthcoming 2010) also concludes that a binding payday loan price cap (36 percent APRs) "harms consumers because it further limits access to credit for many who are already severely credit-constrained, and fails to bring them relief from costly debt" (abstract).

Morgan and Strain (2008) also find that households are not better off without AFS products. They provide evidence that after payday restrictions were imposed in Georgia and North Carolina, households had more bounced checks, had higher rates of complaint to the Federal Trade Commission, and filed for bankruptcy at a higher rate. Finally, Morse (2009) finds that payday lenders offer a positive service to individuals facing financial distress.

Melzer (forthcoming), on the other hand, finds that increased access to payday loans makes it more challenging for families to pay their mortgage, rent, and utility bills, and more likely to delay health care consumption. He concludes that while payday loans might be used to pay for emergency expenditures, the costs of debt servicing worsen various economic outcomes. Skiba and Tobacman (2008) use an alteration in credit score thresholds used for payday loan approval to identify the impact of payday borrowing on Chapter 13 bankruptcy filings. They find that the approval of a payday loan for a first-time applicant increases the rate of bankruptcy by 2.48 percent.

While a number of studies have considered consumer well-being, research has yet to answer whether consumers, on net, benefit from or are harmed by AFS products, even for the most studied product payday loans (Caskey 2010).

When consumers are asked whether they are satisfied with payday and rent-to-own products, a majority report they are. Elliehausen and Lawrence (2001) find that most payday customers believe that people benefit from the use of credit and that payday loan companies provide a useful service. Nonetheless, the majority of customers believe that payday loans are expensive, and a large percentage of customers report that the cost of payday loans is higher than fees for returned checks or late payments on debts. The small percentage of customers who were dissatisfied with their most recent payday loans cited the high cost as the reason for their dissatisfaction. Customers also expressed disagreement with government limits on the number of times a consumer can obtain payday loans during the year. Lacko, McKernan, and Hastak (2002) state that careful analysis should be undertaken before adopting policies that would substantially limit availability of rent-to-own transactions because most (75 percent) rent-to-own customers are satisfied with their experience. Nineteen percent of rent-to-own customers were dissatisfied, with the major complaint being about high prices. Are there other policies that do not restrict access but make consumers better off? Disclosures may be an answer.

Well-designed and -timed disclosures can affect consumer behavior. Another strand of research examines whether AFS disclosures affect consumer behavior and provides suggestive evidence that well-designed and -timed disclosures can affect consumer behavior for some, but not all, consumers. Bertrand and Morse (2010) find that disclosing how the fees accompanying a given payday loan add up over time and disclosing the typical repayment profile of payday loans results in a reduction in the amount of payday borrowing. However, consumers who take up large payday loans (as a fraction of their income) are unaffected by disclosures. The authors suggest that information disclosures might be more effective policy tools if they are combined with well-thought-out regulatory limits on how much people can borrow at interest rates relative to their payback capacity.

McKernan, Lacko, and Hastak (2003) find that state disclosure laws are associated with rent-to-own customers' intention of purchasing or renting from rent-to-own stores. Consumers living in states with total cost label disclosure laws are less likely to use rent-to-own stores to purchase than are consumers living in other states, though this finding is not robust to all model specifications. The authors state that if this finding is reliable, it is consistent with a conclusion that some customers underestimate the cost in the absence of total cost disclosures and that disclosures more fully inform these consumers, leading some to make different decisions. They also find evidence that education (and thus financial literacy) may enable consumers to better assess the cost and make more informed decisions. They recommend that the total cost and other terms of purchase be provided on product labels and in agreements (Lacko, McKernan, and Hastak 2002; McKernan, Lacko, and Hastak 2003).

Fee disclosures may be better than APR disclosures on AFS products. There is also evidence to suggest that fee disclosures are better than APR disclosures on AFS products. AFS consumers may understand fees more easily than APRs on short-term AFS products. Bertrand and Morse (2010) suggest that when customers are informed about the costs of their payday loans in dollar amounts, they reduce borrowing relative to a control group (that receives a standard APR disclosure) by 23 percent.

Elliehausen and Lawrence (2001) find that nearly all payday loan customers were aware of the finance charge for their most recent payday advance, but few were able to report accurate annual percentage rates despite recalling receipt of that information in truth-in-lending disclosures. According to the authors, a likely explanation is that payday loan customers used finance charges rather than annual percentage rates in decisionmaking. Similarly, Elliehausen (2005) finds that most refund anticipation loan customers lack awareness of the APR for their loans. Only about a quarter of refund anticipation loan customers recalled receiving an APR disclosure and of those recalling receipt of an APR, 85 percent said that they did not know the rate. This lack of consumer knowledge suggests that refund anticipation loan customers are unlikely to have found APR information useful in making their decisions.

Lacko, McKernan, and Hastak (2002) state that APR disclosures and price restriction policies in the rent-to-own arena raise more difficult questions than disclosures, because they could be subject to manipulation by rent-to-own dealers. For instance, rent-to-own dealers can inflate the price of the product in order to lower the APR. Anderson and Jackson (2004) find that most rent-to-own merchandise purchases (56 percent) came through early purchase—the customer paid a lump sum to buy before term. Early purchase is generally less expensive than purchasing after renting for the full lease period. Twenty-five percent of purchases (12 percent of all agreements) were made by customers renting to term. Because only 12 percent of all agreements end with the customer renting to term, the authors conclude that APR is not the most useful information for customers. Instead, disclosures should focus on the purchase price at different points in time.

APR (or interest rate) disclosures could be important for longer term loans. Stango and Zinman (2009) provide evidence that APR disclosure regulation, when enforced, does change market outcomes for consumer installment loans.

This paper contributes to the literature by (1) providing a nationally representative picture of the relationship between state AFS policies and consumer product use; (2) measuring this relationship for less studied products, such as auto title and pawnshop loans; (3) looking across five AFS products, rather than at one product in isolation; and (4) examining substitution between AFS products.

III. HOW MIGHT STATE POLICIES AFFECT AFS PRODUCT USE?

State policies can affect both the supply of and the demand for AFS products and thus consumer use of the products. The state policies we examine fall into three categories: prohibitions, price caps, and disclosures. Overall, we expect prohibitions decrease consumer use, price caps either increase or decrease use, and disclosures decrease use. The conceptual framework below suggests these relationships are more complicated than might be expected at first glance. For example, policies will affect many consumers and suppliers beyond those who are directly targeted by policies, partly because there are many possible substitutions between consumers, products, and suppliers.

Prohibitions and price caps. Prohibitions are expected to reduce the quantity supplied and thus consumer use of the product. Consumer use of the product may not go to zero if consumers in a state where the product is prohibited use the product in a nearby state where it is not prohibited or obtain it online.

Price caps could either increase or decrease consumer use of AFS products, depending on whether a demand or supply effect dominates. A price cap, by lowering the price relative to other alternatives, is expected to increase (quantity) demand for the product. The ultimate question is, what do suppliers do? A price cap could decrease (quantity) supply by limiting firm profits. A price cap is also likely to affect market shares, that is, change the make-up of firms supplying AFS. For example, anecdotal evidence suggests that when California implemented its rent-to-own price cap, small "mom and pop" firms, who were no longer profitable with the price cut, went out of business and national chains saw decreased profits but increased revenue from the additional business. A price cap is also likely to change the customers a lender is willing to serve. For example, a price restriction may induce suppliers to shift their clientele to serve less risky, and thus less costly, customers. A lower price may also attract lower credit risk customers. This scenario is less likely in the short run, however, because of the stigma associated with the AFS lenders and products.

Disclosures. Overall we expect clear and timely disclosures to reduce AFS product use, though there are scenarios where use could increase. Disclosure laws may decrease demand for the product by disclosing to consumers the full cost of the transaction. Disclosures may also decrease the supply of the product by increasing dealer costs. Both of these effects would reduce consumer use of the product. Disclosures could also make a market more competitive by allowing consumers to better shop on price. The increased competition could induce suppliers to reduce price or provide better products and service and thus increase demand for the product.

Policy interactions and substitution across product. AFS products can be substitutes for one another. Enforced restriction for one product can increase demand for another product by shifting demand from one product to the other. Evidence of this substitution can be seen in the shift from refund anticipation loans to refund anticipation checks with the 2006 price cap restriction on loans to military personnel (Theodos et al. 2010). At the same time, it is possible that a restriction on one AFS product could decrease use of other AFS products by lowering complementary foot traffic in stores or by lowering profits for dealers that rely on the sale of multiple products to stay in business. Because AFS products often serve the same cash and credit restrained customers, many AFS suppliers offer multiple products within their stores. For example, many pawnbrokers offer payday loans (Caskey 2005) and many rent-to-own stores offer payday loans. And according to Rivlin (2010), "almost every enterprise that's part of the fringe economy takes a stab at the tax return business" (p. 265).

IV. Data

Our study relies on both individual-level survey data and state-level policy and economic data. We discuss each of these in turn below.

National Financial Capability State-by-State Survey

The individual-level data for this study come from the National Financial Capability State-by-State Survey, sponsored by the FINRA Investor Educational Foundation.[5] This Internet-based survey includes roughly 500 respondents per state (plus DC), for a total sample of about 28,000 respondents. When weighted, the data are nationally representative.

The survey was administered in mid-2009 and asks a variety of point-in-time questions about respondents' demographic and financial characteristics, including age, educational attainment, race and ethnicity, living arrangements, number of financially dependent children, income, and banked status.[6] Key for this analysis is retrospective questions that ask respondents if they used each of five AFS products—auto title, payday, pawnshop, refund anticipation loan, and rent-to-own—over the last five years. Because AFS use is measured over the past five years and state of residence is measured at the time of the survey, people who moved across state lines over the past five years may not have used the AFS product in their current state of residence.

In general, item nonresponse was low for most survey questions; roughly 2.5 percent of respondents did not answer the AFS product use questions and so are excluded from the analysis. Overall, our sample includes 27,456 people. Use of AFS products cuts across income group and educational attainment (as described below and in table 2), so all analyses examine the full population.

Use of AFS products. Between 6 percent and 13 percent of the sample reported using each of the five AFS products over the five-year period from mid-2004 through mid-2009. Auto title loans and refund anticipation loans are used least often (6 percent), and pawnshop loans are used most often (13 percent; table 1 last row). The usage rates for payday and pawnshop borrowing are higher than the usage rates found in a companion telephone survey of nearly 1,500 adults—10 versus 5 percent for payday borrowing and 13 versus 8 percent for pawnshop borrowing. An Internet-based survey, such as this one, could produce higher AFS usage rates if respondents are more comfortable reporting AFS usage via an Internet survey than to an interviewer on the telephone.

AFS use varies substantially across states (table 1). For example, payday loans are used by less than 5 percent of the population in five states, but used by more than 15 percent of the population in another five states. Similarly, refund anticipation loan use varies substantially across states, from a low of 2 percent in New Hampshire and Idaho to a high of 15 percent in Mississippi. There is also variation within state across products. For example, no state has the same level of use for each product. Also, while some states have AFS usage rates that are consistently above or below the national average (e.g., Arizona and New Jersey, respectively),

---

[5] FINRA is a registered trademark of the Financial Industry Regulatory Authority.
[6] All questions used for this analysis ask about the individual except for number of financially dependent children (self and spouse/partner), income (household), and banked status (household).

other states have usage rates that are above the national average for some products but below the national average for other products (e.g., Ohio and Washington).

There is some overlap in AFS customers across products, although the majority of AFS customers used only one of the five products during the past five years (58 percent). Beyond this, 25 percent of AFS customers used two products, 11 percent used three products, and the remaining 6 percent used four or five products. Thus, our analyses of the five products capture, in large part, different groups of customers.

Demographic and household characteristics. AFS customers are varied and AFS use cuts across multiple dimensions including income, banked status, age, educational attainment, race, and gender. As compared with non-AFS users, AFS customers do, however, tend be lower income, unbanked, younger, less educated, minority, financially responsible for more children, and to live in the South (table 2)[7]. As noted above, the survey asks about AFS product use over the course of the last five years, while the demographic and household characteristics are measured at the time of the survey. Keeping in mind that some individual and household characteristics may have changed over time, we note some differences in customers of different AFS products.

The five AFS products are used by persons in each of the four income groups, which range from less than $25,000 to $75,000 or more (table 2).[8] Among AFS consumers, pawnshop and rent-to-own customers tend to have the lowest incomes, while auto title customers have higher incomes. For example, 17 percent of auto title customers have household incomes of at least $75,000, as compared with 6 percent of pawnshop and rent-to-own customers. The comparable number for payday and refund anticipation loan customers is 9 percent. Auto title customers, along with payday customers, are also more likely to have a bank account. About 90 percent of auto title and payday customers report having a bank account, while roughly 80 percent of pawnshop, RAL, and rent-to-own customers are banked. Similarly, auto title and payday customers have higher levels of education than do users of the other three products. In all cases, however, persons who did not use an AFS product are on average more advantaged. Minorities are disproportionately more likely to use each of the five AFS products, as are people who live in the South.

State-Level AFS Policy Data

The National Financial Capability State-by-State data are augmented with state-level AFS polices, with information ranging from prohibitions and price caps to disclosure requirements. These policy data were assembled from documents published by a number of organizations including the Consumer Federation of America, the National Conference of State Legislatures, the

---

[7] For the purposes of this analysis, we use the Census designation of the South, which includes Alabama, Arkansas, Delaware, the District of Columbia, Florida, Georgia, Kentucky, Louisiana, Maryland, Mississippi, North Carolina, Oklahoma, South Carolina, Tennessee, Texas, Virginia, and West Virginia.

[8] The survey data provides household income in four discrete ranges: less than $25,000, between $25,000 and $50,000, between $50,000 and $75,000, and $75,000 or more.

National Consumer Law Center, and the Association of Progressive Rental Organizations. In addition, experts in the field reviewed and commented on a preliminary version of these data.[9] Source documentation is available from 2004 through 2009 for only some of the AFS policy variables. In cases where source data are not available for each year and state policies are the same at two points in time (e.g., 2005 and 2008), we assume no change in the interim years. When the policies did change, we obtained follow-up documentation to identify the year in which the policy changed.[10] The data appendix provides detailed information on each policy variable.

Few of the policies changed between mid-2004 and mid-2009. Since the individual-level National Financial Capability State-by-State data capture AFS use at any point over a five year period, we measure each policy with a single variable. Specifically, we take the policy that was in place for the majority of time over the 2004–2009 period.[11]

Table 3 presents a summary of the state policies included in our analysis, by product. Two of the five products, auto title loans and payday loans, have prohibitions in place in some states during the study period. The auto title industry has restrictions in the majority of states, with 26 states prohibiting auto title loans[12] and another 12 states with APR caps.[13] These auto title APR caps range from a low of 21 percent in Iowa to a high of 304 percent in four states—Alabama, Georgia, Mississippi, and Montana. The majority of states also have payday loan restrictions, although only half as many states, 13, prohibit payday loans. Thirty-three states restrict the APR on payday loans, although the average APR cap among these states is high at 487 percent.[14]

Forty states also have a monthly interest rate cap on pawnshop loans. These monthly interest rates range from 1 percent to 25 percent, which translate to APRs of roughly 13 percent to over 1,300 percent. Many fewer states, 11, have rent-to-own APR or other price restrictions.[15]

---

[9] These experts included staff from the Office of the Comptroller of the Currency, the Association of Progressive Rental Organizations, the Center for Responsible Lending, the Conference of State Bank Supervisors, and a national pawnbroker association.

[10] Source data for the pawnshop policy variables were only available for 2005. We did, however, have an expert in the field review these data (see data appendix).

[11] When the policy changed in the middle of the study period, we took the policy that was in place in the latter half of the period.

[12] Texas has statutory prohibitions on auto title loans, but auto title lenders can be active as brokers for unregulated "credit servicing organizations." As a result, we do not treat Texas as prohibiting auto title lending for the purposes of the empirical analysis. This reduces the number of states with auto title prohibitions from 27 to 26.

[13] South Carolina imposes an APR cap of 15 percent but only on loans below $600. Since most auto title loans are larger than $600, we consider the South Carolina cap nonbinding, reducing the number of states recorded in our analysis as having a cap to 12.

[14] These caps ranged from Ohio's 28 percent APR cap to Missouri's 1,980 percent APR cap. Since Missouri's cap is a significant outlier in the data, the empirical analysis sets this to the next highest value, which is 780 percent. Two of the 33 states (Oregon and New Mexico) implemented their payday loan caps in the middle of the study period.

[15] We were unable to identify a continuous measure of state rent-to-own price or APR caps.

In addition to these price restrictions, 10 states require pawnshops to return excess proceeds to the customer upon sale of the collateral. Several states require the disclosure of certain information about refund anticipation loans and/or rent-to-own transactions. Seventeen states require disclosures of a standard set of contract terms for refund anticipation loans. Common refund anticipation loan requirements include disclosures for the loan's APR, loan fee schedule, and filing fees.[16] Forty seven states require rent-to-own providers to disclose contract information, while 16 states take the additional step of requiring total cost label disclosures.[17]

State-Level Economic Data

State-level economic conditions may contribute to AFS product use. People may be more likely to use an AFS product if employment levels are low and the unemployment rate is high, for example. To control for economic conditions, the individual-level data are supplemented with state-level data on (1) real personal income per capita, (2) the unemployment rate, (3) the employment-to-population ratio, and (4) real GDP per capita by state. These data were collected from the U.S. Department of Labor (2010) and the U.S. Department of Commerce (2010a, 2010b, and 2010c). Values for these variables are averaged over the study period and included in the empirical model.[18]

V. EMPIRICAL MODEL

The empirical model measures the relationship between AFS policies and AFS product use, with a focus on five products: auto title loans, payday loans, pawnshop loans, refund anticipation loans, and rent-to-own. We estimate a separate model for each product. Individual-level National Financial Capability State-by-State data are used to capture consumers' use of AFS products in the last five years, as well as their demographic and household characteristics, while the AFS policies are measured at the state level.

We estimate models for AFS use (Y_{is}) for person i in state s:

$$Y_{is} = \alpha + \delta' AFS_s + \beta_1' X_{is} + \beta_2' S_s + v_{is}.$$

Using auto title as an example, Y_{is} indicates whether person i who lives in state s at the time of the survey took out an auto title loan in the past five years (yes=1, no=0). In this case, AFS_s represents the state-level auto title policies for each person in the sample. X_{is} represents individual demographic characteristics and household composition variables, including age, educational attainment, race and ethnicity, gender, living arrangement, number of financially dependent children, and region. S_s represents state-level economic variables including per capita

---

[16] Three states impose APR caps on RALs; these caps are not included in our analyses because of the limited variation across states.

[17] The correlation in state policies across the AFS products is always below 0.55 and is generally below 0.40. The highest degree of correlation is between states that restrict auto title and pay day loans at 0.55.

[18] The employment-to-population ratio and real GDP per capita by state are only available through 2008.

income, unemployment rate, employment-to-population ratio, and per capita gross domestic product (GDP) by state. We estimate additional specifications that include income and bank status; the estimated relationship between AFS policies and AFS product use in the alternate specifications are virtually identical to the main results. v_{is} is the error term. We estimate weighted probit models and cluster the standard errors by state to account for potential serial correlation in the error term (Bertrand et al. 2004).

Our model is identified by variation across states only. It does not include a time element because the individual-level National Financial Capability State-by-State data only capture whether respondents used the specific AFS products at any point over the five-year period from mid-2004 to mid-2009. We do not have information, for example, on whether respondents used the products in *each* of the five years. The cross-sectional nature of these data is a limitation for our analysis. If the data captured AFS use at multiple points in time, we could use the variation to estimate a cleaner relationship between AFS policies and AFS use.[19] With our specification, we measure the *relationship* between AFS policies and AFS product use; we do not measure the causal impact of AFS policies on product use. Nonetheless, the results do provide information on how AFS policies relate to AFS product use, controlling for important individual- and family-level characteristics as well as state-level economic conditions.

There can be important differences between the intent of a policy and how it is implemented and used in practice. As discussed in the literature review, suppliers may find ways to circumvent policies by altering their products. This would lessen the impact of the policy on product use. Also, with national chains, laws in some states can affect policies in all states. For example, Rent-A-Center provides total cost label disclosures in all states, irrespective of the state law, because some states require it. While we expect this type of response to increase the potential impact of the policy on product use, it decreases the measured relationship between the policy change and product use. Thus, our analysis captures the relationship between AFS use and AFS policies as they are implemented and used in practice; we do not necessarily measure the relationship that captures the intent of the law.

Interpreting the Model Coefficients

The estimated coefficients from the probit models do not have a straightforward interpretation. To present a clear interpretation of the results, we use the estimated coefficients to calculate the associated change in the probability of using an AFS product when the AFS policy changes. For example, we calculate how moving from no APR cap to an APR cap of 36 percent relates to auto title borrowing by calculating (1) the average of each individual's likelihood of auto title borrowing *when the state has no APR cap*, (2) the average of each individual's likelihood of auto title borrowing *when the state has a 36 percent APR cap*, and (3) the difference between these

---

[19] In this case, models would include, at a minimum, state fixed effects and time fixed effects (as done in much of the welfare reform literature).

two average likelihoods.[20] This difference provides an estimate of the relationship between the AFS policy change and AFS product use, and is referred to as the "simulated probability."

VI. RESULTS

What Is the Relationship between State-Level AFS Policies and AFS Use?

Price Caps and Prohibitions

The results suggest that more stringent price caps and prohibitions are often associated with lower AFS product use. We find this relationship for three of the products—auto title, payday, and pawnshop loans. We do not, however, find evidence that price caps are associated with lower rent-to-own use. Our analysis does not consider the relationship between refund anticipation loan price caps and refund anticipation loan use, since there is not enough variation across states to estimate the relationship—only three states impose price caps on refund anticipation loans.

As discussed above, restricting the loan price can have two offsetting effects. A lower-priced loan is expected to increase the (quantity) demand for the loan, but can increase or decrease the (quantity) supply of the loan. Suppliers would only meet the increased consumer demand if there were some excess profit, non-competitive pricing by some suppliers, or other limitations in the prior market. Our finding that more stringent price caps are indeed associated with lower AFS product use suggests that the decrease in supply dominates. That is, the increase in demand for the product does not prompt an increase in total supply. In fact, the results suggest that providers provide less (i.e., reduce supply). Restrictions on the price lenders are allowed to charge for a loan can decrease the supply of the loan product if, for example, small firms are no longer profitable and leave the industry.

Auto title loans. We measure auto title loan policies with three variables: APR cap amount and two indicator variables that capture whether the state has no price cap and whether the state prohibits auto title loans. The coefficients on the price cap amount and the indicator of no price cap are statistically significantly different from zero (p=0.00 and p=0.06, respectively), while the coefficient on the prohibited variable is not statistically significantly different from zero (p=0.15: table 4, column 1).

Interpreting these three variables in conjunction with one another, we find that moving from an APR cap of 200 percent to 100 percent is associated with a 1.5 percentage point (21 percent) reduction in the use of auto title borrowing (table 4, column 2). The FDIC's model for small-dollar loans suggests an APR of 36 percent or less. Using this as a guide, we examine a change

---

[20] For each product, the estimated probability that individual *i* uses the product is expressed as $\Phi(\hat{\alpha} + \hat{\delta}'AFS_s + \hat{\beta}_1'X_{is} + \hat{\beta}_2'S_s)$, where Φ represents the cumulative normal distribution and $\hat{\alpha}$, $\hat{\delta}$, $\hat{\beta}_1$, *and* $\hat{\beta}_2$ are the estimated coefficient from the probit model.

15

from no APR cap to an APR cap of 36 percent and find that such a change is associated with a 2.0 percentage point reduction in auto title borrowing (not shown). This represents a 30 percent decline, from 6.8 percent to 4.8 percent.

A 30 percent decline is substantial, yet one might expect this APR restriction to be associated with even larger declines in auto title borrowing. Auto suppliers might exclude higher risk borrowers, thereby lowering their own net costs of supplying this borrowing to those who remain. Also, as discussed above, analyses of the auto title industry have found that auto title lenders use loan structures to circumvent rate caps (Fox and Guy 2005; Feltner 2007). For example, some auto title lenders have been found to repackage single-payment auto title loans as lines of credit in order to skirt interest rate caps (Fox and Guy 2005).

We do find a negative and statistically significant coefficient (p=0.06) on the no price cap indicator variable. This finding suggests a lower use of auto title loans for persons in states with no price cap than for persons in states with the highest APR cap of 304 percent. It is not clear why the relationship is negative. It seems more likely an artifact of the data or empirical model than a true finding, but is worthy of future investigation, e.g., do a few states with no price cap still provide lower net costs for consumers through competitive markets.

Payday loans. We measure payday loan policies with the same three variables: an indicator of whether the state prohibits payday loans, the APR cap amount, and an indicator of no APR price cap. The results suggest that prohibiting payday lending is the key policy associated with the use of payday loans. The coefficients on the APR cap amount and the indicator of no APR price cap are not statistically significantly different from zero. Focusing in on the prohibition variable, we find that that prohibiting payday loans is associated with a 3.4 percentage point reduction in payday borrowing, which represents a 35 percent decline in this type of borrowing (table 4, columns 3–4).[21] Living in a state that prohibits payday lending does not necessarily prevent residents of that state from getting a payday loan. People that live near the border with another state can go across state lines to obtain a payday loan. Also, Internet payday loans are generally available to people who live in states that prohibit payday lending businesses.

Unlike the auto title loan results, we do not find that a reduction in the payday loan APR cap (beyond prohibiting the product) is associated with reduced use. Over the 2005–2009 period covered by this analysis, 33 states had an APR cap on payday loans, although the majority of these caps were set upwards of 300 percent. Payday loans often cost about $15 per $100 borrowed, which translates into a 390 percent APR. Among the 33 states with a payday cap, only four states had an APR cap below 390 percent. The relatively limited variation in the APR

---

[21] This simulated effect is calculated at the mean for all other variables, including the price cap amount and price cap dummy variables. We do this to isolate the effect of prohibiting payday lending, since the price cap amount and price cap dummy variables are not statistically significantly different from zero. We estimated an additional model that includes only to prohibit variables (i.e., excluded the price cap amount and price cap dummy variables) and find consistent results—prohibiting payday lending is associated with a one third decline in use of payday loans.

caps in the range where these caps are more likely to be binding may account for our statistically insignificant finding.

Our finding that prohibiting payday loans is associated with lower consumer use is broadly consistent with other studies that suggest tighter restrictions on the payday industry lower payday borrowing by lowering supply (Dunham forthcoming 2010; Prager 2009; Zinman 2010). For example, Zinman's (2010) study of payday lending in Washington and Oregon finds that the likelihood of payday borrowing fell by roughly one-third in Oregon, relative to Washington, when Oregon imposed a 150 percent payday cap (Washington had an APR cap of 390 percent).

Pawnshop. No state prohibits pawnshops, so we focus on whether the state has a price cap and the cap amount. Pawnshop price caps are measured as a monthly interest rate cap, and range from 1 percent to 25 percent in the 40 states that impose a cap. Monthly interest rates in this range translate into APRs of roughly 13 percent to over 1,300 percent. With these high interest rate ceilings, it is not surprising that we find no statistically significant difference in pawnshop borrowing when there is no interest rate cap versus when the interest rate cap is set at the maximum of 25 percent.

The cap does matter, however, when it is lowered further. Consistent with the auto title results, we find that more restrictive price caps are associated with less borrowing. Moving from a price cap of 10 percent to 5 percent, for example, is associated with a 0.6 percentage point (or 6 percent) reduction in pawnshop borrowing (table 4, columns 5–6). Larger changes are, of course, associated with larger declines in use. Moving from no interest rate cap to a cap of 3 percent (roughly a 40 percent APR) is associated with a 3.1 percentage point (or 25 percent) reduction in pawnshop borrowing (not shown).

Rent-to-own. We capture rent-to-own price restrictions with a single indicator variable that identifies whether the state had an APR or total cost price cap in place during the 2004–2009 study period. Over this five-year period, 10 states impose total cost price caps, while one state (MN) had an APR price cap.[22] Unlike our analysis of the three loan products, we find no statistically significant relationship between rent-to-own price caps and use of rent-to-own. We were not able to collect the same level of detail on the price cap amounts, which may help explain our lack of finding here.

Return Requirements and Disclosures

We examine pawnshop return requirements and disclosure requirements for refund anticipation loans and rent-to-own. Our analysis provides little evidence that these requirements are related to AFS product use. APR disclosures may have little relationship to AFS use if the APR disclosure is not meaningful to consumers on short-term AFS products. If customers do not understand what an APR represents, for example, then disclosing this

---

[22] With the exception of California, the price cap policies were in place across the five-year period. California instituted total cost price cap rules in 2007.

information is not likely to influence behavior. Earlier studies do, in fact, find that many AFS customers lack of awareness about their loan APR (Elliehausen 2005; Elliehausen and Lawrence 2001). However, disclosing more specific information about how the cost of a payday loan can add up over time (Bertrand and Morse 2010) and the total cost of using rent-to-own to purchase an item (McKernan, Lacko, and Hastak 2003) has been found to reduce product use. With our broad sweep of five AFS products and use of national-level data, we are not able to drill down to the level of detail of some of these earlier studies.

Pawnshops. Our analysis of pawnshop borrowing includes an indicator variable that identifies whether states require pawnshops to return to the borrower excess proceeds from the sale of the item used for collateral. Ten states have such a requirement. All else equal, this policy reduces the expected payoff to the loan provider, so loan amounts are expected to fall. A fall in the loan amount relative to the value of the collateralized item may reduce pawnshop borrowing. However, the policy could have little effect on pawnshop use if borrowers expect to repay the loan. We find no evidence that return requirements are associated with the level of pawnshop borrowing (table 4, column 5–6).

Refund anticipation loans. We find no evidence that refund anticipation (RAL) disclosure requirements are associated with lower RAL use. While the estimated coefficient is negative, it is not statistically significantly different from zero (table 4, columns 7–8). RAL disclosure requirements vary across the 17 states that have such requirements, although common requirements include disclosure of the loan's APR, tax preparation fees, loan fee schedules, filing fees, and information on alternative e-filing options.

Rent-to-own. Our results suggest that requiring rent-to-own businesses to disclose standard information on the product contract is associated with greater use of rent-to-own. Specifically, requiring contract disclosures is associated with the 1.9 percentage point increase in the likelihood of using rent-to-own. While we generally expect disclosures to reduce use, they could increase use in the longer run by making the market more competitive—allowing consumers to better shop on price and removing high-priced suppliers. We find no evidence that total cost label disclosures are significantly related to rent-to-own use. Prior research suggests that these disclosures are associated with lower use among customers who use rent-to-own with the intent to purchase (McKernan et al. 2003). These authors do not find evidence that total cost price disclosures are significantly related to rent-to-own use among customers who use rent-to-own with the intent to rent only. The individual-level data used for this analysis do not provide information on the intent of rent-to-own customers (to purchase or rent), so we are not able to disentangle the different relationships.

Are Restrictions on One AFS Product Associated with Increased Use of Other AFS Products?

Here we examine whether prohibiting or strictly enforcing price caps on one AFS product is associated with increased use of another product. For example, are tight restrictions on payday lending associated with greater use of auto title loans? We estimate the same models as presented in table 4, but also include policy variables of other products. The auto title loan model, for example, includes measures of payday, pawnshop, and rent-to-own policies. With a focus on prohibitions and price caps, the cross-product policy variables included in the models are (1) auto title loans prohibited or have an APR cap of less than or equal to 36 percent (0/1 indicator variable), (2) payday loans prohibited or have an APR cap of less than or equal to 36 percent (0/1), (3) pawnshop loans have a monthly interest rate cap of less than or equal to 3 percent (0/1),[23] and (4) rent-to-own industry has price caps.

When we add these additional policy variables to the models, the estimated relationships for the existing variables are similar to those shown in table 4. For this reason, the discussion below focuses on the cross-product variables.

Overall, our results do not support the hypothesis that prohibitions and price caps on one AFS product lead consumers to use other AFS products. Among the cross-product policy variables in the five models, we find only one statistically significant relationship (table 5, bottom panel).[24] Stricter auto title loan policies are associated with greater use of rent-to-own transactions. Based on the number of cross-product policy variables (16 in the five models) and the level of statistical significance we examine (10 percent), we would expect one or two (1.6, to be precise) policy variables to be statistically significant just by chance. For this reason, we do not put much weight on the one statistically significant relationship.

Our finding that prohibitions and price caps on one AFS product do not necessarily lead consumers to use other AFS products is consistent with Zinman (2010), who finds no evidence that payday restrictions in Oregon led to increased use of auto title loans, although he does not examine substitutions between other AFS products. Zinman does, however, find evidence of a substitution between payday loans and both checking account overdrafts and late bill payment, both of which can have substantial costs. Additional research on how consumers meet their credit needs when government policies restrict the supply of AFS products, and the implications for consumer welfare, will help policymakers assess the costs and benefits of restrictions on AFS products.

How Are Demographic and Economic Characteristics Related to the Use of AFS Products?

Consistent with descriptive analyses, results from the multivariate analysis show AFS users tend to be young, less educated, minority, living in a cohabiting relationship or living alone, financially responsible for more children, and living in the South (table 4, second panel).

---

[23] Recall that no state prohibits pawnshop loans and that a monthly interest rate cap of 3 percent translates to an APR near 36 percent (43 percent).

[24] The lack of statistical significance does not appear to be driven by multicollinearity; the highest correlation between these policies is 0.37.

As compared with persons ages 45 to 54, those under age 45 are generally more likely to use each of the five AFS products, while those over age 55 are less likely to use the AFS products (although not all the coefficients are statistically significantly different from zero at the 10 percent level). One exception is that persons ages 18 to 24 are 2.9 percentage point less to use payday loans than those ages 45 to 54. This is likely due to the fact that payday customers must have a regular job, since the person's next paycheck secures the loan. Educational attainment is also a factor, particularly for pawnshop borrowing and the use of rent-to-own. In both cases, persons with a high school diploma are 6.6 percentage points less likely to use these products, as compared with persons with no high school diploma. The likelihood of using these products falls precipitously with higher levels of educational attainment. This statistically significant pattern holds in models that include household income and banked status, although the differences between educational groups are smaller (see appendix table A.1). Notably, there is no statistically significant difference in auto title borrowing by educational attainment.

African-Americans are more likely than whites to use each of the five AFS products. At the low end of the range, they are 1.9 percentage points more likely to take an auto title loan, and at the high end, they are 8.2 percentage points more likely to take out a payday loan. The magnitudes of these differences are only slightly lower in models that include income and banked status. In general men and women use these products at similar levels, although the results suggest that females are 0.8 percentage points less likely to take out an auto title loan.

Living arrangements and the number of financially dependent children also play a role. As compared with married couple families, single people who live with a parent are 2.1 to 3.4 percentage points less likely to use each of the AFS products. On the other hand, persons in cohabiting relationships and single people who live with others (i.e., with nonparents) are more likely to use four of the five AFS products (payday loans, pawnshop loans, refund anticipation loans, and rent-to-own). Living with others may, in particular, signal economic distress. Being financially responsible for an additional child is associated with an increased likelihood of using the AFS products of between 1.0 and 1.7 percentage points.

Our analysis also examines region and state economic conditions. As compared with persons living in the South, those in the Northeast are less likely to take out payday loans, pawnshop loans, and refund anticipation loans, while those in the Midwest[25] are less likely to take out pawnshop loans. In general, we find a limited relationship between state economic characteristics and use of AFS products, except for real personal per capita income. We find that a $5,000 increase in per capita income is associated with a 1.2 percentage point decline in the

---

[25] We use the Census designation of the Northeast, which includes Connecticut, Maine, Massachusetts, New Hampshire, New Jersey, New York, Pennsylvania, Rhode Island, and Vermont. We also use the Census designation of the Midwest, which includes Illinois, Indiana, Iowa, Kansas, Michigan, Minnesota, Missouri, Nebraska, North Dakota, Ohio, South Dakota, and Wisconsin.

likelihood of auto title or payday borrowing and a 1.5 percentage point decline in the likelihood of using rent-to-own.

VII. Policy Implications

Price caps and prohibitions on AFS products are associated with reduced supply. Restricting supply can increase well-being when it restricts or exposes high-priced suppliers who might be offering products at well-above-market prices. At the same time, restricting supply without introducing alternative products can reduce consumer well-being, as consumers turn to inferior products or options to deal with credit needs. Encouraging alternative products—products that are less costly and more attractive than those currently available—is likely to enhance consumer well-being, especially if it helps create a more competitive market for services.

The FDIC small-dollar loan pilot program might be thought of as an approach that tries to negotiate various concerns. In pilot efforts, financial institutions were encouraged to set the APR no higher than 36 percent. In the end, however, while some banks in the pilot were able to provide profitable small-dollar loans, others were not (Federal Deposit Insurance Corporation 2010). Encouraging mainstream financial institutions to provide small-dollar loans but easing the 36 percent APR cap may prompt more banks to provide small-dollar loans to higher-risk consumers that rely on AFS products. In addition, small-dollar loans could be more profitable if financial institutions provide customers with a line of credit, rather than having to originate a new loan each time the person needs credit.

Findings from the literature suggest that standard, clear, and timely disclosures of the total cost of short-term, small-dollar products will help consumers know their full obligations, so that they can more easily compare what various providers charge for their loans and services. Disclosures may not always reduce demand, but they may help consumers avoid higher-priced suppliers (e.g., those with misleading advertising). Improved disclosures could increase competition within the alternative financial sector, reducing prices for consumers. And full disclosures, along with licensing, reporting, and examination requirements, could enhance the industry's image and make the small loan business more appealing to both mainstream and alternative entrants.

VIII. Summary and Conclusion

This study uses new nationally representative data from the National Financial Capability State-by-State Survey to examine the relationship between state-level AFS policies (prohibitions, price caps, disclosures) and consumer use of five AFS products: payday loans, auto title loans, pawnshop loans, refund anticipation loans, and rent-to-own transactions. Looking across products rather than at one product in isolation allows a focus on patterns and relationships across products.

The results suggest that more stringent price caps and prohibitions are associated with lower consumer product use. Specifically, we find prohibiting payday loans is associated with a 35 percent decline in the use of these loans. Further, we find that price caps are associated with reduced use of auto title loans and pawnshop loans. Moving from no APR cap on auto title loans to an APR cap of 36 percent is associated with a 30 percent decline in auto title borrowing. Similarly, moving from no interest rate cap on pawnshop loans to a monthly interest rate of 3 percent (which is roughly a 40 percent APR) is associated with a 25 percent decline in pawnshop borrowing.

Lower levels of use, which likely result from reduced supply, could potentially worsen consumer well-being as consumers turn to potentially inferior alternatives. To address this question, we examine whether consumers, when faced with restrictions on one AFS product move to use other AFS products. We find no evidence that prohibitions and price caps on one AFS product lead consumers to use other AFS products. While other studies have also found no substitution between AFS products, a recent study finds evidence of a substitution between payday loans and both checking account overdrafts and late bill payment, both of which can have substantial costs (Zinman 2010).

Finally, our analysis examines disclosure requirements for refund anticipation loans and rent-to-own and finds little evidence that these requirements are related to AFS product use. Our findings may be a result of data limitations, as other studies suggest that clear and timely disclosures reduce AFS product use.

This paper provides a first look at a nationally representative picture of the relationship between state AFS policies and consumer product use across five AFS products. This research provides a course for future research, which could examine the less-studied AFS products and across multiple products to (1) measure the causal impact of AFS policies on consumer outcomes (e.g., by using quasi-experimental methods and longitudinal data or experimental methods); (2) uncover how the effect of state AFS policies on AFS product use differ among consumers along important dimensions such as education, income, and financial stress; (3) design and test effective disclosures for AFS products and customers; and (4) research how AFS policies affect consumer well-being. Research has yet to answer whether consumers, on net, benefit from or are harmed by alternative AFS products, even for the most studied product payday loans (Caskey 2010). With respect to this last question, important distinctions need to be made as to whether the products themselves are harmful per se, particular suppliers of the product are charging excessive prices or misleading consumers, or particular consumers are harmed by participating in this market. Also, we need to better understand any impact on higher-risk consumers who might be further excluded, and lower-risk consumers, who could end up with better prices.

REFERENCES

Anderson, M. H., and R. Jackson. 2004. "Rent-to-Own Agreements: Purchases or Rentals?" *Journal of Applied Business Research* 20(1): 13–22.

Barr, Michael. 2004. "Banking the Poor." *Yale Journal on Regulation* 21:127–237.

Bertrand, Marianne, and Adair Morse. 2010. "Information Disclosure, Cognitive Biases, and Payday Borrowing." Working paper. Chicago, IL: Booth School of Business, University of Chicago.

Bertrand, Marianne, Esther Duflo, and Sendhil Mullainathan. 2004. "How Much Should We Trust Differences-in-Differences Estimates?" *Quarterly Journal of Economics* 119(1): 249–75.

Caskey, John. 1994. *Fringe Banking: Check Cashing Outlets, Pawnshops and the Poor*. New York: Russell Sage Foundation.

Caskey, John. 2005. "Fringe Banking and the Rise of Payday Lending." In *Credit Markets for the Poor,* edited by P. Bolton and H. Rosenthal (17–45). New York: Russell Sage Foundation.

———. 2010. "Payday Lending: New Research and the Big Question." Working paper 10-32. Philadelphia: Research Department, Federal Reserve Bank of Philadelphia.

Dunham, Constance R. Forthcoming 2010. "A 36 Percent Price Cap on Consumer Credit: How Do Payday Loan Customers Fare?" Washington, DC: Office of the Comptroller of the Currency.

Elliehausen, Gregory. 2005. "Consumer Use of Tax Refund Anticipation Loans". Working paper. Washington, DC: Credit Research Center, Georgetown University.

Elliehausen, Gregory, and Edward Lawrence. 2001. "Payday Advance Credit in America: An Analysis of Customer Demand." Working paper. Washington, DC: Credit Research Center, Georgetown University.

Federal Deposit Insurance Corporation. 2010. "A Template for Success: The FDIC's Small-Dollar Loan Pilot Program." *Federal Deposit Insurance Corporation Quarterly* 4(2): 28–41.

Fellowes, Matt, and Mia Mabanta. 2008. "Banking on Wealth: America's New Retail Banking Infrastructure and Its Wealth-Building Potential." Research Brief. Washington, DC: Brookings Institution.

Feltner, Tom. 2007. "Debt Detour: The Automobile Title Lending Industry in Illinois." Chicago, IL: Woodstock Institute and the Public Action Foundation.

Flannery, Mark, and Katherine Samolyk. 2005. "Payday Lending: Do the Costs Justify the Price?" Center for Financial Research Working Paper 2005-09. Washington, DC: FDIC.

Fox, Jean Ann, and Elizabeth Guy. 2005. "Driven into Debt: CFA Car Title Loan Store and Online Survey." Washington, DC: Consumer Federation of America.

Lacko, James, Signe-Mary McKernan, and Manoj Hastak. 2002. "Customer Experience with Rent-to-Own Transactions." *Journal of Public Policy and Marketing* 21(1): 126–38.

McKernan, Signe-Mary, and Caroline Ratcliffe. 2008. "Enabling Families to Weather Emergencies and Develop: The Role of Assets." New Safety Net Paper 7. Washington, DC: The Urban Institute.

McKernan, Signe-Mary, James Lacko, and Manoj Hastak. 2003. "Empirical Evidence on the Determinant of Rent-to-Own Use and Purchase Behavior." *Economic Development Quarterly* 17(1): 33–52.

Melzer, Brian. Forthcoming. "The Real Costs of Credit Access: Evidence from the Payday Loan Market." *Quarterly Journal of Economics*.

Morgan, Donald, and Michael Strain. 2008. "Payday Holiday: How Households Fare after Payday Credit Bans." Staff report 309. New York: New York Federal Reserve.

Morse, Adair. 2009. "Payday Lenders: Heroes or Villains?" Working paper. Chicago, IL: University of Chicago.

National Pawnbrokers Association. 2008. "Pawnbroking Industry Overview: Meeting the Needs of America's Working Families." Keller, TX: National Pawnbrokers Association.

Prager, R. A. 2009. "Determinants of the Locations of Payday Lenders, Pawnshops, and Check-Cashing Outlets." Washington, DC: Federal Reserve Board.

Rivlin, Gary. 2010. *Broke, USA: From Pawnshops to Poverty, Inc.—How the Working Poor Became Big Business*. New York: HarperCollins Publishers.

Skiba, P., and J. Tobacman. 2007. "The Profitability of Payday Loans." Working paper. Nashville, TN: Vanderbilt University.

———. 2008. "Do Payday Loans Cause Bankruptcy?" Working paper. Philadelphia: University of Pennsylvania.

South Carolina Appleseed Legal Justice Center. 2004. "Auto Title Loans and the Law." Columbia, SC: South Carolina Appleseed Legal Justice Center.

Stango, V., and J. Zinman. 2009. "Fuzzy Math, Disclosure Regulation, and Credit Market Outcomes: Evidence from Truth-in-Lending Reform." Working paper. Davis, CA: U. C. Davis.

Stegman, Michael. 2007. "Payday Lending." *Journal of Economic Perspectives* 21: 169–90.

Theodos, Brett, and Jessica Compton. 2010. "Research on Financial Behaviors and Use of Small-Dollar Loans and Financial Services." Washington, DC: The Urban Institute.

Theodos, Brett, Rachel Brash, Jessica Compton, Karen Masken, Nancy Pindus, and C. Eugene Steuerle. 2010. "Who Needs Credit at Tax Time and Why." Washington, DC: The Urban Institute.

U.S. Department of Commerce, Bureau of Economic Analysis, Regional Economic Accounts. 2010a. "Regional Economic Accounts, per capita real GDP by state." http://www.bea.gov/regional/gsp. (Accessed July 1, 2010.)

U.S. Department of Commerce, Bureau of Economic Analysis, Regional Economic Accounts. 2010b. "Regional Economic Accounts, per capita personal income by state." http://www.bea.gov/regional/spi. (Accessed July 1, 2010.)

U.S. Department of Commerce, Census Bureau. 2010c. "Population, population change and estimated components of population change: April 1, 2000 to July 1, 2009." http://www.census.gov/popest/national/files/NST_EST2009_ALLDATA.csv. (Accessed July 1, 2010.)

U.S. Department of Labor, Bureau of Labor Statistics. 2010. "Local Area Unemployment Statistics." http://data.bls.gov:8080/PDQ/outside.jsp?survey=la. (Accessed July 1, 2010.)

Zinman, Jonathan. 2010. "Restricting Consumer Credit Access: Household Survey Evidence on Effects around the Oregon Rate Cap." *Journal of Banking and Finance* 34(3).

Table 1: Percent of Population that Used AFS Products in the Last Five Years

	Auto Title	Payday	Pawnshop	Refund Anticipation Loan	Rent-to-Own
Alabama	11%	12%	20%	10%	12%
Alaska	6%	11%	15%	5%	7%
Arizona	10%	18%	24%	12%	13%
Arkansas	4%	9%	19%	9%	15%
California	5%	8%	9%	3%	3%
Colorado	7%	12%	16%	4%	6%
Connecticut	4%	4%	12%	5%	10%
Delaware	6%	8%	7%	4%	8%
District of Columbia	4%	15%	11%	9%	3%
Florida	4%	11%	17%	7%	6%
Georgia	9%	6%	15%	7%	7%
Hawaii	5%	13%	7%	7%	8%
Idaho	8%	12%	14%	2%	6%
Illinois	3%	9%	10%	5%	5%
Indiana	7%	11%	14%	7%	10%
Iowa	8%	8%	10%	5%	7%
Kansas	7%	10%	13%	5%	10%
Kentucky	7%	11%	17%	11%	14%
Louisiana	7%	13%	13%	8%	10%
Maine	6%	4%	11%	5%	10%
Maryland	4%	7%	14%	6%	6%
Massachusetts	3%	3%	9%	3%	6%
Michigan	4%	7%	9%	6%	4%
Minnesota	5%	5%	17%	4%	1%
Mississippi	15%	13%	18%	15%	16%
Missouri	6%	11%	14%	7%	9%
Montana	12%	19%	22%	6%	7%
Nebraska	6%	10%	10%	4%	8%
Nevada	6%	21%	18%	8%	6%
New Hampshire	4%	5%	7%	2%	6%
New Jersey	4%	3%	7%	5%	4%
New Mexico	10%	15%	13%	7%	7%
New York	5%	4%	11%	5%	6%
North Carolina	7%	4%	17%	9%	9%
North Dakota	9%	10%	13%	4%	6%
Ohio	5%	12%	9%	8%	9%
Oklahoma	10%	14%	20%	7%	10%
Oregon	4%	10%	13%	5%	7%
Pennsylvania	5%	5%	6%	4%	6%
Rhode Island	8%	6%	11%	6%	9%
South Carolina	12%	17%	24%	9%	10%
South Dakota	9%	13%	14%	6%	6%
Tennessee	10%	14%	16%	13%	11%
Texas	8%	13%	26%	9%	11%
Utah	9%	13%	15%	3%	6%
Vermont	7%	4%	3%	3%	9%
Virginia	6%	9%	12%	6%	5%
Washington	5%	13%	17%	6%	8%
West Virginia	6%	7%	16%	9%	9%
Wisconsin	7%	9%	8%	3%	4%
Wyoming	12%	17%	24%	10%	8%
Total	**6%**	**10%**	**13%**	**6%**	**8%**

Source: Authors' tabulations of the National Financial Capability State-by-State Survey

Table 2: Individual Demographic and Household Characteristics by AFS Use

	Auto Title	Payday	Pawnshop	Refund Anticipation Loan	Rent-to-Own	No AFS Use	Total
Household Income							
< $25,000	31%	39%	53%	42%	48%	27%	32%
$25,000–$49,999	34%	37%	30%	36%	35%	27%	28%
$50,000–$74,999	17%	15%	11%	13%	11%	19%	17%
≥ $75,000	17%	9%	6%	9%	6%	27%	23%
Family is banked	92%	89%	79%	80%	83%	95%	92%
Age							
18–24	11%	10%	24%	13%	18%	11%	13%
25–34	27%	27%	25%	37%	27%	15%	17%
35–44	23%	26%	24%	29%	26%	17%	19%
45–54	19%	22%	17%	14%	18%	20%	20%
55–64	11%	10%	7%	4%	7%	17%	15%
65 ≥	9%	5%	3%	3%	4%	21%	17%
Education							
Less than high school	16%	21%	30%	26%	34%	12%	15%
High school graduate	34%	32%	33%	35%	32%	27%	29%
Some college	31%	33%	27%	28%	25%	31%	31%
College degree	19%	14%	10%	11%	9%	30%	25%
Race							
White	64%	56%	56%	55%	58%	72%	69%
Black	16%	22%	19%	22%	20%	9%	11%
Hispanic	13%	16%	20%	17%	14%	12%	13%
Other	7%	7%	6%	5%	7%	7%	6%
Female	50%	54%	51%	54%	55%	51%	51%
Living Arrangements							
Married	56%	47%	38%	50%	49%	55%	53%
Cohabiting	13%	15%	15%	16%	16%	7%	8%
Single, living alone	17%	22%	20%	19%	17%	22%	22%
Single, living with a parent	5%	5%	14%	6%	6%	8%	8%
Single, living with other	9%	10%	12%	10%	12%	8%	9%
Number of financially dependent children	1.2	1.3	1.1	1.6	1.4	0.6	0.8
Region							
South	43%	41%	46%	47%	46%	34%	37%
Northeast	14%	8%	12%	13%	15%	20%	18%
Midwest	20%	22%	18%	19%	19%	23%	22%
West	23%	29%	24%	20%	20%	23%	23%
Observations	1,761	2,524	3,157	1,470	1,717	21,003	27,456

Source: Author's calculations from the National Financial Capability State-by-State Survey.

Notes: Average state economic conditions over the study period are included in the regressions but not shown in this table. The mean values for these variables for the full sample are state real personal income per capita, $31,507; state unemployment rate, 5.7%; state employment-to-population ratio, 71.7%; real GDP per capita by state, $37,860.

Table 3: State Alternative Financial Service Policies by Product

	Number of States	Mean	Min	Max
Auto Title Loan				
Product Prohibited	26	51%	0%	1
APR price cap	12	24%	0%	1
APR price cap amount	12	174%	21%	304%
Payday Loan				
Product Prohibited	13	26%	0	1
APR price cap	33	64%	0	1
APR price cap amount	33	487%	28%	780%[5]
Pawnshop Loan				
Monthly interest rate price cap	40	78%	0	1
Monthly interest rate price cap amount	40	14%	1%	25%
Return requirement[1]	10	20%	0	1
Refund Anticipation Loan				
Disclosure requirement[2]	14	22%	0	1
Rent-to-Own				
Price or APR cap	11	21%	0	1
Contract disclosures[3]	47	92%	0	1
Total cost label disclosures[4]	16	31%	0	1

Source: Authors' calculations from policy data assembled from documents published by the Consumer Federation of America, the National Conference of State Legislatures, the National Consumer Law Center, and the Association of Progressive Rental Organizations. In addition, experts reviewed and commented on a preliminary version of these data.

[1] States with return requirements require the pawnshop to return excess proceeds to the customer upon sale of collateral.

[2] Refund anticipation loan disclosure requirements vary across states. A standard core of disclosure requirements including the loan's APR, tax preparation fees, and fee schedules was required in almost all states. More detailed disclosure requirements were also enacted, including font size requirements and posting requirements.

[3] Rent-to-own contract dislosures require rent-to-own businesses to provide standard information on the product contract.

[4] Rent-to-own total cost label disclosures require rent-to-own businesses to disclose the total cost of purchase on the product label.

[5] Missouri reports an APR cap of 1,980 percent. Since this is a significant outlier in the data, the empirical analysis sets this to the next highest value, which is 780 percent.

Table 4: Probit Model Estimates of the Relationship between AFS Policies and AFS Product Use

Policy Variables	Auto Title		Payday		Pawnshop		Refund Anticipation Loan		Rent-to-Own	
	Coeff./ st. error	Simulated Probability	Coeff./ st. error	Simulated Probability	Coeff./ st. error	Simulated Probability	Coeff./ st. error	Simulated Probability	Coeff./ st. error	Simulated Probability
Price caps and prohibitions										
Product prohibited (0/1)[1]	0.149 [0.104]	1.1	-0.249** [0.102]	-3.4						
No price cap (0/1)[2]	-0.149* [0.079]	-2.1	-0.051 [0.161]	-0.8	0.023 [0.072]	0.4			0.093 [0.062]	1.0
Price cap amount (%/100)[3]	0.124*** [0.035]	1.5	-0.005 [0.014]	-0.1	0.736* [0.402]	0.6				
Disclosures and other requirements										
Return requirement (0/1)					0.002 [0.078]	0.0				
Contract disclosures (0/1)							-0.067 [0.053]	-0.6	0.202** [0.088]	1.9
Total cost label disclosures (0/1)									-0.014 [0.055]	-0.2
Demographic and Family Characteristics (0/1: Omitted, 45–54)										
18–24	0.048 [0.079]	0.6	-0.202*** [0.061]	-2.9	0.378*** [0.056]	7.6	0.219*** [0.083]	2.0	0.274*** [0.088]	3.5
25–34	0.227*** [0.050]	3.1	0.118** [0.051]	2.1	0.272*** [0.057]	5.2	0.517*** [0.063]	5.9	0.236*** [0.061]	2.9
35–44	0.069 [0.052]	0.8	0.043 [0.054]	0.7	0.199*** [0.057]	3.6	0.306*** [0.066]	3.0	0.158*** [0.055]	1.9
55–64	-0.066 [0.045]	-0.7	-0.205*** [0.050]	-3.0	-0.233*** [0.054]	-3.3	-0.314*** [0.065]	-1.8	-0.215*** [0.062]	-1.9
65 and older	-0.204*** [0.066]	-2.0	-0.580*** [0.071]	-6.6	-0.763*** [0.087]	-7.6	-0.501*** [0.092]	-2.5	-0.592*** [0.098]	-0.4
Education (0/1: Omitted, less than high school)										
High school graduate	0.130 [0.084]	1.7	-0.045 [0.059]	-0.8	-0.271*** [0.052]	-6.6	-0.075 [0.092]	1.0	-0.353*** [0.061]	-6.6
Some college	0.038 [0.084]	0.5	-0.118* [0.063]	-2.1	-0.445*** [0.057]	-10.1	-0.235*** [0.086]	-2.9	-0.550*** [0.055]	-9.2
College or more	-0.104 [0.092]	-1.1	-0.452*** [0.074]	-6.6	-0.828*** [0.060]	-15.8	-0.624*** [0.088]	-6.0	-0.907*** [0.065]	-12.4

continued

29

Table 4, continued: Probit Model Estimates of the Relationship between AFS Policies and AFS Product Use

	Auto Title		Payday		Pawnshop		Refund Anticipation Loan		Rent-to-Own	
	Coeff./ st. error	Simulated Probability	Coeff./ st. error	Simulated Probability	Coeff./ st. error	Simulated Probability	Coeff./ st. error	Simulated Probability	Coeff./ st. error	Simulated Probability
Race/Ethnicity (0/1: Omitted, white)										
Black	0.144** [0.060]	1.9	0.456*** [0.049]	8.2	0.274*** [0.057]	5.1	0.307*** [0.053]	3.4	0.301*** [0.066]	3.8
Hispanic	-0.028 [0.050]	-0.3	0.062 [0.052]	0.9	0.095 [0.065]	1.6	0.027 [0.071]	0.2	-0.073 [0.065]	-0.7
Other	0.073 [0.097]	0.9	0.099 [0.073]	1.4	-0.002 [0.075]	-0.0	0.025 [0.149]	0.2	0.172* [0.090]	2.0
Female	-0.064** [0.030]	-0.8	0.002 [0.041]	0.0	-0.032 [0.027]	-0.5	-0.018 [0.045]	-0.2	0.021 [0.039]	0.2
Living arrangement (Omitted: married)										
Cohabiting	0.094 [0.062]	1.3	0.291*** [0.072]	4.8	0.332*** [0.066]	5.9	0.135** [0.057]	1.4	0.154** [0.065]	1.9
Single, live alone	-0.081 [0.051]	-1.0	0.158*** [0.044]	2.4	0.230*** [0.050]	3.8	0.062 [0.062]	0.6	-0.006 [0.057]	-0.1
Single, live with parent	-0.332*** [0.077]	-3.2	-0.187** [0.080]	-2.3	0.205*** [0.070]	3.4	-0.276*** [0.098]	-2.1	-0.390*** [0.099]	-3.2
Single, live with other	0.000 [0.060]	0.0	0.195*** [0.057]	3.0	0.342*** [0.057]	6.1	0.111* [0.064]	1.1	0.161** [0.076]	2.0
Number of financially dependent children (0–4)[4]	0.084*** [0.015]	1.1	0.125*** [0.016]	2.0	0.094*** [0.013]	1.7	0.184*** [0.017]	2.0	0.132*** [0.017]	1.6
Region (0/1: Omitted, South)										
Northeast	-0.020 [0.068]	-0.3	-0.219*** [0.077]	-2.8	-0.346*** [0.102]	-5.6	-0.170*** [0.051]	-1.5	0.113 [0.083]	1.3
Midwest	-0.090 [0.097]	-1.1	-0.005 [0.069]	-0.1	-0.259*** [0.087]	-4.4	-0.047 [0.062]	-0.5	-0.033 [0.075]	-0.4
West	-0.026 [0.059]	-0.3	0.123** [0.057]	2.0	-0.080 [0.085]	-1.5	-0.113 [0.073]	-1.1	-0.068 [0.062]	-0.7

continued

30

Table 4, continued: Probit Model Estimates of the Relationship between AFS Policies and AFS Product Use

	Auto Title		Payday		Pawnshop		Refund Anticipation Loan		Rent-to-Own	
	Coeff./ st. error	Simulated Probability	Coeff./ st. error	Simulated Probability	Coeff./ st. error	Simulated Probability	Coeff./ st. error	Simulated Probability	Coeff./ st. error	Simulated Probability
State Economic Characteristics[5]										
Real personal income per capita ($1,000)	-0.020** [0.009]	-1.2	-0.017* [0.010]	-1.2	0.000 [0.011]	0.000	-0.006 [0.010]	-0.3	-0.030*** [0.009]	-1.5
Unemployment rate (%)	-0.022 [0.027]	-0.3	-0.038 [0.031]	-0.6	0.016 [0.038]	0.003	0.010 [0.024]	0.1	-0.038 [0.027]	-0.4
Employment-to-population ratio (%)	0.008 [0.009]	0.0	0.005 [0.008]	0.0	0.010 [0.010]	0.000	-0.012 [0.008]	-0.0	-0.005 [0.008]	-0.0
Real GDP per capita for ($1,000)	0.001 [0.003]	0.0	0.005 [0.004]	0.4	-0.004 [0.004]	-0.004	0.001 [0.004]	0.0	0.003 [0.003]	0.2
Constant	-1.597** [0.670]		-1.074* [0.602]		-1.676** [0.832]		-0.716 [0.541]		0.022 [0.717]	
Observations	27,456		27,456		27,456		27,456		27,456	

Notes: Robust standard errors are in brackets. Simulated probabilities are the estimated percentage point change in the likelihood of using an AFS product when the explanatory variable changes. For most variables, the simulated effects are calculated going from 0 to 1. The exceptions are described in the notes below. We estimate additional specifications that include income and banked status; the estimated relationship between AFS policies and AFS product use in the alternate specifications are virtually identical to the main results and are presented in appendix table A-1.

[1] Simulating probabilities associated with product prohibitions requires changes in the price cap amount. When prohibition is changed from 0 to 1, price cap amounts change from 36% to 0% for auto title and payday loan use.

[2] Simulating probabilities associated with price cap requires assumptions about the price cap amount. When the "no cap" indicator is changed from 0 to 1, price cap amounts remain at the highest price cap in the sample, which is 304% for auto title loans, 780% for payday loans, and 25% for pawnshop loans.

[3] To simulate probabilities associated with the price cap amount, the cap is changed from 100% to 200% for auto title and payday loans and from 5% to 10% for pawnshop loans.

[4] To simulate probabilities associated with the number of financially dependent children, the number is assumed to change from one to two.

[5] For state economic characteristics, we use the mean of each variable as a guide for calculating the simulated probability. The simulated changes are as follows: (1) real personal income per capita changes from $30,000 to $35,000, (2) the unemployment rate, from 5% to 6%, (3) the employment-to-population ratio, from 70% to 75%, and (4) real gross domestic product (GDP) by state per capita from $35,000 to $40,000.

*** p<0.01, ** p<0.05, * p<0.1

31

Table 5: Probit Model Estimates of the Relationship between AFS Policies and AFS Product Use, with Cross-Product Relationships

	Auto Title		Payday		Pawnshop		Refund Anticipation Loan		Rent-to-Own	
Policy Variables	Coeff/ st error	Simulated Probability	Coeff/ st error	Simulated Probability	Coeff/ st error	Simulated Probability	Coeff/ st error	Simulated Probability	Coeff/ st error	Simulated Probability
Price caps and prohibitions										
Product prohibited (0/1)[1]	0.173* [0.104]	1.3	-0.232** [0.115]	-3.2						
No price cap (0/1)[2]	-0.148** [0.075]	-2.1	-0.046 [0.152]	-0.7	0.064 [0.073]	1.2			0.143* [0.074]	1.5
Price cap amount (%/100)[3]	0.129*** [0.034]	1.5	-0.006 [0.016]	-0.1	0.619* [0.369]	1.0				
Disclosures and other requirements										
Return requirement (0/1)					-0.002 [0.073]	-0.0				
Contract disclosures (0/1)							-0.032 [0.055]	-0.3	0.214* [0.118]	2.0
Total cost label disclosures (0/1)									0.004 [0.075]	0.0
Cross-Product Policy Variables										
Prohibited or strict price cap										
Auto title: prohibited or APR cap ≤ 36%			-0.015 [0.047]	-0.2	0.013 [0.052]	0.2	0.026 [0.047]	0.3	0.100** [0.043]	1.1
Payday: prohibited or APR cap ≤ 36%	-0.042 [0.053]	-0.5			-0.083 [0.054]	-1.4	-0.009 [0.054]	-0.1	-0.005 [0.103]	-0.1
Pawnshop: prohibited or interest rate ≤ 3%	-0.089 [0.104]	-1.0	-0.075 [0.079]	-1.1			-0.092 [0.059]	-0.8	0.077 [0.047]	0.9
Price cap indicator										
RTO: price cap indicator (0/1)	-0.014 [0.048]	-0.2	-0.062 [0.057]	-0.9	-0.081 [0.088]	-1.3	0.031 [0.060]	0.3		
Observations	27,456		27,456		27,456		27,456		27,456	

Notes: Robust standard errors are in brackets. Simulated effects are the estimated percentage point change in the likelihood of using an AFS product when the explanatory variable changes. For most variables the simulated effects are calculated going from 0 to 1. The exception are described in the notes below. The models control for age, education level, race/ethnicity, gender, living arrangement, number of financially dependent children, region, state real personal income per capita, the state unemployment rate, the state employment-to-population ratio, and state real GDP per capita

[1] Simulating probabilities associated with product prohibitions requires changes in the price cap amount. When prohibition is changed from 0 to 1, price cap amounts change from 36% to 0% for auto title and payday loan use

[2] Simulating probabilities associated with price cap requires assumptions about the price cap amount. When the "no cap" indicator is changed from 0 to 1, price cap amounts remain at the highest price cap in the sample, which is 304% for auto title loans, 780% for payday loans, and 25% for pawnshop loans

[3] To simulate probabilities associated with the price cap amount, the cap is changed from 100% to 200% for auto title and payday loans and from 5% to 10% for pawnshop loans

*** p<0.01, ** p<0.05, * p<0.1

Appendix A1: Probit Model Estimates of the Relationship between AFS Policies and AFS Product Use (models include income and banked status)

	Auto Title	Payday	Pawnshop	Refund Anticipation Loan	Rent–to–Own
Policy Variables	Coefficient/ st. error	Coefficient/ st. error	Coefficient/ st. error	Coefficient/ st. error	Coefficient/ st. error
Price caps and prohibitions					
Product prohibited (0/1)	0.151	−0.256**			
	[0.105]	[0.100]			
No price cap (0/1)	−0.154*	−0.014	0.029		0.102
	[0.080]	[0.152]	[0.071]		[0.067]
Price cap amount (%/100)	0.125***	−0.007	0.763*		
	[0.036]	[0.013]	[0.412]		
Disclosures and other requirements					
Return requirement (0/1)			0.027		
			[0.078]		
Contract disclosures (0/1)				−0.077	0.195**
				[0.054]	[0.076]
Total cost label disclosures (0/1)					-0.001
					[0.058]
Demographic Characteristics					
Age (0/1: Omitted, age 45–54)					
Age 18–24	0.046	-0.247***	0.310***	0.162**	0.227***
	[0.081]	[0.063]	[0.062]	[0.081]	[0.088]
Age 25–34	0.213***	0.090*	0.229***	0.488***	0.205***
	[0.051]	[0.052]	[0.057]	[0.065]	[0.060]
Age 35–44	0.068	0.042	0.205***	0.293***	0.163***
	[0.050]	[0.055]	[0.058]	[0.066]	[0.054]
Age 55–64	-0.068	-0.226***	-0.225***	-0.313***	-0.210***
	[0.046]	[0.051]	[0.054]	[0.066]	[0.065]
Age 65 and older	-0.214***	-0.614***	-0.745***	-0.528***	-0.597***
	[0.069]	[0.071]	[0.088]	[0.090]	[0.100]
Education (0/1: Omitted, less than high school)					
High school graduate	0.109	-0.014	-0.123**	0.017	-0.273***
	[0.087]	[0.061]	[0.058]	[0.096]	[0.065]
Some college	0.025	-0.041	-0.213***	-0.091	-0.419***
	[0.085]	[0.066]	[0.063]	[0.092]	[0.063]
College or more	-0.080	-0.252***	-0.440***	-0.376***	-0.623***
	[0.094]	[0.076]	[0.067]	[0.092]	[0.068]
Race/Ethnicity (0/1: Omitted, white)					
Black	0 139**	0.435***	0.230***	0.289***	0.259***
	[0.063]	[0.050]	[0.062]	[0.054]	[0.068]
Hispanic	-0.037	0.029	0.059	-0.014	-0.115
	[0.050]	[0.057]	[0.068]	[0.074]	[0.070]
Other	0.054	0.105	-0.018	0.026	0.146*
	[0.088]	[0.072]	[0.069]	[0.141]	[0.086]
Female	-0.068**	-0.020	-0.063**	-0.044	-0.003
	[0.028]	[0.040]	[0.029]	[0.046]	[0.042]

continued

Appendix A1, continued: Probit Model Estimates of the Relationship between AFS Policies and AFS Product Use (models include income and banked status)

	Auto Title	Payday	Pawnshop	Refund Anticipation Loan	Rent-to-Own
	Coefficient/ st. error	Coefficient/ st. error	Coefficient/ st. error	Coefficient/ st. error	Coefficient/ st. error
Living arrangement (0/1: Omitted, married)					
Cohabiting	0.085	0.221***	0.268***	0.084	0.094
	[0.062]	[0.069]	[0.067]	[0.057]	[0.064]
Single, live alone	-0.095*	0.039	0.033	-0.053	-0.142***
	[0.055]	[0.043]	[0.052]	[0.064]	[0.054]
Single, live with parent	-0.355***	-0.261***	0.047	-0.410***	-0.484***
	[0.086]	[0.080]	[0.071]	[0.097]	[0.102]
Single, live with other	-0.015	0.093	0.143***	-0.010	0.021
	[0.062]	[0.057]	[0.055]	[0.064]	[0.080]
Number of financially dependent	0.085***	0.128***	0.094***	0.180***	0.139***
children (0–4)	[0.015]	[0.015]	[0.013]	[0.017]	[0.017]
Region (0/1: Omitted, South)					
Northeast	-0.031	-0.247***	-0.397***	-0.193***	0.080
	[0.064]	[0.074]	[0.112]	[0.054]	[0.087]
Midwest	-0.102	0.001	-0.267***	-0.052	-0.026
	[0.099]	[0.068]	[0.094]	[0.063]	[0.077]
West	-0.027	0.118**	-0.078	-0.110	-0.067
	[0.059]	[0.055]	[0.085]	[0.076]	[0.062]
State Economic Characteristics					
Real personal income per capita	-0.018**	-0.008	0.007	-0.001	-0.023**
($1,000)	[0.009]	[0.010]	[0.011]	[0.010]	[0.009]
Unemployment rate (%)	-0.019	-0.038	0.020	0.018	-0.040
	[0.027]	[0.030]	[0.039]	[0.025]	[0.028]
Employment–to–population ratio (%)	0.008	0.003	0.012	-0.011	-0.006
	[0.009]	[0.007]	[0.011]	[0.008]	[0.009]
Real GDP per capita for ($1,000)	0.000	0.003	-0.005	0.000	0.002
	[0.003]	[0.004]	[0.003]	[0.003]	[0.003]
Household income (0/1: Omitted, less than $25,000)					
$25,000–$50,000	0.063	0.020	-0.136***	0.050	-0.043
	[0.048]	[0.040]	[0.048]	[0.057]	[0.052]
$50,000–$75,000	-0.020	-0.211***	-0.374***	-0.203***	-0.303***
	[0.053]	[0.044]	[0.056]	[0.063]	[0.057]
$75,000 and greater	-0.109*	-0.537***	-0.718***	-0.387***	-0.642***
	[0.066]	[0.053]	[0.077]	[0.083]	[0.082]
Family is banked (has savings account,	0.057	0.011	-0.383***	-0.336***	-0.103
or a debit or credit card, 0/1)	[0.077]	[0.086]	[0.070]	[0.067]	[0.092]
Constant	-1.738**	-1.008*	-1.538*	-0.643	0.140
	[0.680]	[0.594]	[0.873]	[0.574]	[0.787]
Observations	27,184	27,184	27,184	27,184	27,184

Note: Robust standard errors are in brackets

*** p<0 01, ** p<0 05, * p<0 1

Data Appendix

State auto title loan restrictions

1.   Auto title loans prohibited

   Sources: Fox and Guy, "Driven into Debt: CFA Car Title Loan Store and Online Survey" (2005); Consumers Union, National Consumer Law Center, and Consumer Federation of America, "Small-Dollar Loan Products Scorecard" (2008).

   Variable Type: Binary.

   Values: 0/1 (no/yes): If the state prohibits lenders from making auto title loans, the variable receives a 1; if not, it receives a 0.

   Years Available: 2005, 2008, 2010. The Consumer Federation of America provides data on auto title loan restriction as of 2005. Information on state law as of 2008 is provided by the Consumer Federation of America and the National Consumer Law Center. In 2010, reviewers from the Conference of State Bank Supervisors and the Center for Responsible Lending reviewed the data and advised us on the identification of states where auto title restrictions were nonbinding or circumvented by suppliers.

   Notes: We make the assumption that if auto title loan restrictions in 2008 are identical to the restrictions for 2005 and the reviewers provided no additional information that a change occurred, then these restrictions were also in effect for all intervening years. We also assume that the 2005 restrictions were in place in 2004. Texas has statutory prohibitions on auto title loans, but auto title lenders can be active as brokers for unregulated "credit servicing organizations." As a result, we do not treat Texas as prohibiting auto title lending.

2.   APR cap on auto title loans

   Sources: Fox and Guy, "Driven into Debt: CFA Car Title Loan Store and Online Survey" (2005); Consumers Union, National Consumer Law Center, and Consumer Federation of America, "Small-Dollar Loan Products Scorecard" (2008).

   Variable Type: Continuous.

   Values: A continuous APR cap for states that have a rate cap.

   Years Available: 2005, 2008, 2010. The Consumer Federation of America provides data on auto title loan restriction as of 2005. Information on state law as of 2008 is provided by the Consumer Federation of America and the National Consumer Law Center. In 2010, reviewers from the Conference of State Bank Supervisors and the Center for Responsible Lending reviewed the data and advised us on the identification of states where auto title restrictions were nonbinding or circumvented by suppliers.

   Assumptions: Calculations assume a one-month, $300 auto title loan.

   Notes: We make the assumption that if auto title loan restrictions in 2008 are identical to the restrictions for 2005 and the reviewers provided no additional information that a change occurred, then these restrictions were also in effect for all intervening years. We also assume that the 2005 restrictions were in place in 2004. South Carolina imposes an APR cap of 15 percent but only on loans below $600. Since most auto title loans are larger than $600, we treat South Carolina as having no APR cap.

3.   Auto title loan—no APR cap

Sources: Fox and Guy, "Driven into Debt: CFA Car Title Loan Store and Online Survey" (2005); Consumers Union, National Consumer Law Center, and Consumer Federation of America, "Small-Dollar Loan Products Scorecard" (2008).

Variable Type: Binary.

Values: 0/1 (no/yes): If the state prohibits auto title loans or has an APR cap, the variable receives a 0; if not, it receives a 1.

Years Available: 2005, 2008, 2010. The Consumer Federation of America provides data on auto title loan restriction as of 2005. Information on state law as of 2008 is provided by the Consumer Federation of America and the National Consumer Law Center. In 2010, reviewers from the Conference of State Bank Supervisors and the Center for Responsible Lending reviewed the data and advised us on the identification of states where auto title restrictions were nonbinding or circumvented by suppliers.

Notes: See notes for variables "auto title loans prohibited" and "APR cap on auto title loans" above.

State payday loan restrictions

1.   Payday loans prohibited

Sources: National Consumer Law Center, "Survey of State Payday Loan Laws" (2005); National Conference of State Legislatures, "Payday Lending State Statutes" (2009).

Variable Type: Binary.

Values: 0/1 (no/yes): If the state prohibits lenders from making payday loans, the variable receives a 1; if not, it receives a 0.

Years Available: 2005, 2009, 2010. The National Consumer Law Center provides data on payday loan restriction as of 2005. Information on state law as of 2009 is provided by the National Conference of State Legislatures. In 2010, reviewers from the Conference of State Bank Supervisors and the Treasury Department reviewed the data and advised us on the identification of states where payday restrictions had changed during the study period.

Notes: We make the assumption that if payday loan restrictions in 2009 are identical to the restrictions for 2005 and the reviewers provided no additional information that a change occurred, then these restrictions were also in effect for all intervening years. We also assume that the 2005 restrictions were in place in 2004.

2.   APR cap amount on payday loans

Sources: National Consumer Law Center, "Survey of State Payday Loan Laws" (2005); National Conference of State Legislatures, "Payday Lending State Statutes" (2009); Consumer Federation of America, "Payday Loan Consumer Information: State Information" (2010).

Variable Type: Continuous.

Values: A continuous APR cap for states that have a cap.

Years Available: 2005, 2009, 2010. The National Consumer Law Center provides data on payday loan restriction as of 2005. Information on state law as of 2009 is provided by the National Conference of State Legislatures. In 2010, reviewers from the Conference of State Bank Supervisors and the Treasury Department reviewed the data and advised us on the identification of states where payday restrictions had changed during the study period.

Assumption: Calculations assume a 14 day, $100 payday loan.

Notes:　　We make the assumption that if payday loan restrictions in 2009 are identical to the restrictions for 2005 and the reviewers provided no additional information that a change occurred, then these restrictions were also in effect for all intervening years. We also assume that the 2005 policies were in place in 2004. Some states did change their payday loan restrictions during the study period. In these cases, we conferred with reviewers and with the state code to determine the timing and nature of the change. The Consumer Federation of America (2010) translates the mix of finance charge caps, interest rate caps, and APR caps provided by the National Consumer Law Center into consistently defined APR caps.

3.　　　Payday loan – no APR cap

Sources:　　National Consumer Law Center, "Survey of State Payday Loan Laws" (2005); National Conference of State Legislatures, "Payday Lending State Statutes" (2009).

Variable Type: Binary.

Values:　　0/1 (no/yes): If the state prohibits payday loans or has an APR cap, the variable receives a 0; if not, it receives a 1.

Years Available: 2005, 2009, 2010. The National Consumer Law Center provides data on payday loan restriction as of 2005. Information on state law as of 2009 is provided by the National Conference of State Legislatures. In 2010, reviewers from the Conference of State Bank Supervisors and the Treasury Department reviewed the data and advised us on the identification of states where payday restrictions had changed during the study period. Some states did change their payday loan restrictions during the study period. In these cases, we conferred with reviewers and with the state code to determine the timing and nature of the change.

Notes:　　See notes for variables "payday loans prohibited" and "APR cap amount on payday loans" above.

State pawnshop restrictions

1.　　　Pawnshop monthly interest rate cap amount

Source:　　Shackman and Tenney, "The Effects of Government Regulations on the Supply of Pawn Loans: Evidence from 51 Jurisdictions in the U.S." (2006).

Variable Type: Continuous.

Values:　　A continuous interest rate cap for states that have a rate cap.

Years Available: 2005, 2010. Shackman and Tenney (2006) provide information on state caps on monthly interest rates for pawn loans in 2005. In 2010, a reviewer from a national pawnbroker association advised that the Shackman and Tenney (2006) data are generally current.

Notes:　　Based on the 2010 reviewer comments, we assume that the 2005 policies were in place across the 2004 to 2009 study period.

2.　　　Pawnshop monthly interest rate – no cap

Source:　　Shackman and Tenney, "The Effects of Government Regulations on the Supply of Pawn Loans: Evidence from 51 Jurisdictions in the U.S." (2006).

Variable Type: Binary.

Values: 0/1 (no/yes): If the state has an interest rate cap, the variable receives a 0; if not, it receives a 1.

Years Available: 2005, 2010. Shackman and Tenney (2006) provide information on state caps on monthly interest rates for pawn loans in 2005. In 2010, a reviewer from a national pawnbroker association advised that the Shackman and Tenney (2006) data are generally current.

Notes: Based on the 2010 reviewer comments, we assume that the 2005 policies were in place across the 2004 to 2009 study period.

3.   Pawnshop return requirement

Source: Shackman and Tenney, "The Effects of Government Regulations on the Supply of Pawn Loans: Evidence from 51 Jurisdictions in the U.S." (2006).

Variable Type: Binary.

Values: 0/1 (no/yes): If the state requires the pawnshop to return excess proceeds upon sale of collateral, the variable receives a 1; if not, it receives a 0.

Years Available: 2005, 2010. Shackman and Tenney (2006) provide information on state caps on return requirements for pawn loans in 2005. In 2010, a reviewer from a national pawnbroker association advised that the Shackman and Tenney (2006) data are generally current.

Notes: Based on the 2010 reviewer comments, we assume that the 2005 policies were in place across the 2004 to 2009 study period.

State refund anticipation loan (RAL) restrictions

1.   Refund anticipation loan disclosure requirement

Sources: Wu and Fox (2004, 2005, 2007, 2008, and 2009); Wu, Fox, and Woodall (2006).

Variable Type: Binary.

Values: 0/1 (no/yes): If the state has rules requiring disclosure of loan information, the variable receives a 1; if not, it receives a 0.

Years Available: 2004-2010. In addition to the sources listed above, reviewers from the Conference of State Bank Supervisors and the Treasury Department reviewed the data in 2010.

Notes: Disclosure requirements vary across states. The most common requirements were for the disclosure of the loan's APR, tax preparation fees, loan fee schedules, filing fees, and information on alternative e-filing options. More detailed disclosure requirements were also enacted, including font size requirements and posting requirements. A standard core of disclosure requirements is shared by almost all states. Since variations in additional requirements beyond this core are generally more trivial (i.e., font requirements), all disclosure requirements were condensed into a single disclosure measure.

State rent-to-own (RTO) restrictions

1.   Rent-to-own total cost price cap

Sources: Data from McKernan, Lacko, and Hastak for "Empirical Evidence on the Determinants of
          Rent-to-Own Use and Purchase Agreements" (2003); Association of Progressive Rental
          Organizations, "State Rent-to-Own Statutes and Economic Impact" (2009)
          (http://www.rtohq.org/apro-state-rent-to-own-statutes-and-economic-impact.html)
          and "RTO Legislative Activity" (2010) (http://www.rtohq.org/apro-rent-to-own-
          legislative-activity-and-resources.html).

Variable Type: Binary.

Values: 0/1 (no/yes): If the state limits the amount rent-to-own businesses can charge for a
          product, the variable receives a 1; if not, it receives a 0.

Years Available: 2003, 2009, 2010. McKernan et al. (2003) provides data on rent-to-own restrictions
          as of 2003. Retrospective information on state law as of 2009 is provided by the
          Association of Progressive Rental Owners (APRO) at http://www.rtohq.org. In 2010,
          reviewers from the Conference of State Bank Supervisors and APRO reviewed the data
          and advised us on the identification of states where rent-to-own restrictions had
          changed during the study period. APRO's state legislative updates (2010) are also used
          to identify any changes in this state restriction between 2003 and 2009.

Notes: If the APRO legislative updates do not show any changes from 2003, we make the
          assumption that the rent-to-own restrictions were also in effect for all intervening years.
          Some states did change their rent-to-own price cap restrictions during the study period.
          In these cases, we conferred with reviewers to determine the timing and nature of the
          change.

2.   Rent-to-own APR price cap

Sources: Data from McKernan, Lacko, and Hastak for "Empirical Evidence on the Determinants of
          Rent-to-Own Use and Purchase Agreements" (2003); Association of Progressive Rental
          Organizations, "State Rent-to-Own Statutes and Economic Impact" (2009)
          (http://www.rtohq.org/apro-state-rent-to-own-statutes-and-economic-impact.html)
          and "RTO Legislative Activity" (2010) (http://www.rtohq.org/apro-rent-to-own-
          legislative-activity-and-resources.html).

Variable Type: Binary.

Values: 0/1 (no/yes): If the state limits the APR rent-to-own businesses can charge for a product,
          the variable receives a 1; if not, it receives a 0.

Years Available: 2003, 2009, 2010. McKernan et al. (2003) provides data on rent-to-own restrictions
          as of 2003. Retrospective information on state law as of 2009 is provided by the
          Association of Progressive Rental Owners (APRO) at http://www.rtohq.org. In 2010,
          reviewers from the Conference of State Bank Supervisors and APRO reviewed the data.
          APRO's state legislative updates (2010) are also used to identify any changes in this state
          restriction between 2003 and 2009.

Notes: The APRO legislative updates do not show any changes during the study period; we
          make the assumption that these restrictions were in effect for all intervening years.

3.   Rent-to-own contract disclosures

Sources: Data from McKernan, Lacko, and Hastak for "Empirical Evidence on the Determinants of Rent-to-Own Use and Purchase Agreements" (2003); Association of Progressive Rental Organizations, "State Rent-to-Own Statutes and Economic Impact" (2009) (http://www.rtohq.org/apro-state-rent-to-own-statutes-and-economic-impact.html) and "RTO Legislative Activity" (2010) (http://www.rtohq.org/apro-rent-to-own-legislative-activity-and-resources.html).

Variable Type: Binary.

Values: 0/1 (no/yes): If the state requires a lessor to provide standard information on the product contract, the variable receives a 1; if not, it receives a 0.

Years Available: 2003, 2009, 2010. McKernan et al. (2003) provides data on rent-to-own restrictions as of 2003. Retrospective information on state law as of 2009 is provided by the Association of Progressive Rental Owners (APRO) at http"//www.rtohq.org. In 2010, reviewers from the Conference of State Bank Supervisors and APRO reviewed the data. APRO's state legislative updates (2010) are also used to identify any changes in this state restriction between 2003 and 2009.

Notes: The APRO legislative updates do not show any changes during the study period; we make the assumption that these restrictions were in effect for all intervening years.

4.   Rent-to-own total cost label disclosures

Sources: Data from McKernan, Lacko, and Hastak for "Empirical Evidence on the Determinants of Rent-to-Own Use and Purchase Agreements" (2003); Association of Progressive Rental Organizations, "State Rent-to-Own Statutes and Economic Impact" (2009) (http://www.rtohq.org/apro-state-rent-to-own-statutes-and-economic-impact.html) and "RTO Legislative Activity" (2010) (http://www.rtohq.org/apro-rent-to-own-legislative-activity-and-resources.html).

Variable Type: Binary.

Values: 0/1 (no/yes): If the state requires rent-to-own businesses to disclose the total cost of purchase on the product label, the variable receives a 1; if not, it receives a 0.

Years Available: 2003, 2009, 2010. McKernan et al. (2003) provides data on rent-to-own restrictions as of 2003. Retrospective information on state law as of 2009 is provided by the Association of Progressive Rental Owners (APRO) at http://www.rtohq.org. In 2010, reviewers from the Conference of State Bank Supervisors and APRO reviewed the data. APRO's state legislative updates (2010) are also used to identify any changes in this state restriction between 2003 and 2009.

Notes: The APRO legislative updates do not show any changes during the study period; we make the assumption that these restrictions were in effect for all intervening years.

Sources for state policies

Association of Progressive Rental Organizations. 2009. "State Rent-to-Own Statutes and Economic Impact." Austin, TX.

———. 2010. "RTO Legislative Activity." Austin, TX.

Conference of State Bank Supervisors. 2010. Data provided to the Urban Institute.

California Financial Code, Sections 22250-22251. 2010. Accessed at http://law.justia.com/california/codes/fin/22300-22342.html on May 25, 2010.

Consumer Federation of America. 2010. "Payday Loan Consumer Information: State Information." Washington, DC. Accessed at http://www.paydayloaninfo.org/stateinfo.asp on August 4, 2010.

Consumers Union, the National Consumer Law Center, and the Consumer Federation of America. 2008. "Small-Dollar Loan Products Scorecard: Statutory Backup" Washington, DC.

Fox, Jean Ann, and Elizabeth Guy. 2005. "Driven into Debt: CFA Car Title Loan Store and Online Survey." Washington, DC.: Consumer Federation of America.

McKernan, Signe-Mary, James M. Lacko, and Manoj Hastak. 2003. "Empirical Evidence on the Determinants of Rent-to-Own Use and Purchase Agreements." *Economic Development Quarterly* 17(1): 33–52.

National Conference of State Legislatures. 2009. "Payday Lending State Statutes." Denver, CO.

National Consumer Law Center. 2005. "Survey of State Payday Loan Laws." Washington, DC.

Shackman, Joshua, and Glen Tenney. 2006. "The Effects of Government Regulations on the Supply of Pawn Loans: Evidence from 51 Jurisdictions in the U.S." *Journal of Financial Services Review* 30(2): 69–91.

South Carolina Code of Laws (Unannotated), Current through the end of the 2009 Session. 2010. Accessed at http://www.scstatehouse.gov/code/t37c003.htm on April 6, 2010.

Wu, Chi Chi, and Jean Ann Fox. 2004. "All Drain, No Gain: Refund Anticipation Loans Continue to Sap the Hard-Earned Tax Dollars of Low-Income Americans." NCLC/CFA 2004 Refund Anticipation Loan Report. Washington, DC: National Consumer Law Center and Consumer Federation of America.

———. 2005. "Picking Taxpayers' Pockets, Draining Tax Relief Dollars: Refund Anticipation Loans Still Slicing into Low-Income Americans' Hard-Earned Tax Refunds." NCLC/CFA 2005 Refund Anticipation Loan Report. Washington, DC: National Consumer Law Center and Consumer Federation of America.

———. 2007. "One Step Forward, One Step Back: Progress Seen in Efforts gainst High-Priced Refund Anticipation Loans, but Even More Abusive Products Introduced." NCLC/CFA 2007 Refund

Anticipation Loan Report. Washington, DC: National Consumer Law Center and Consumer Federation of America.

———. 2008. "Coming Down: Fewer Refund Anticipation Loans, Lower Prices from Some Providers, but Quickie Tax Refund Loans Still Burden the Working Poor." NCLC/CFA 2008 Refund Anticipation Loan Report. Washington, DC: National Consumer Law Center and Consumer Federation of America.

———. 2009. "Big Business, Big Bucks: Quickie Tax Loans Generate Profits for Banks and Tax Preparers while Putting Low-Income Taxpayers at Risk." NCLC/CFA 2009 Refund Anticipation Loan Report. Washington, DC: National Consumer Law Center and Consumer Federation of America.

———. 2010. "Major Changes in the Quick Tax Refund Loan Industry." NCLC/CFA 2010 Refund Anticipation Loan Report. Washington, DC: National Consumer Law Center and Consumer Federation of America.

Wu, Chi Chi, Jean Ann Fox, and Patrick Woodall. 2006. "Another Year of Losses: High-Priced Refund Anticipation Loans Continue to Take a Chunk out of Americans' Tax Refunds." NCLC/CFA 2006 Refund Anticipation Loan Report. Washington, DC: National Consumer Law Center and Consumer Federation of America.

www.ingramcontent.com/pod-product-compliance
Lightning Source LLC
Chambersburg PA
CBHW052019280526
45793CB00005B/1047